NINJA FOODI GRILL COOKBOOK FOR BEGINNERS

BY
JIM WANG

Copyright 2020 - All rights reserved.

The trademarks that are used are without any consent, and the publication of the trademark is without permission or backing by the trademark owner. All trademarks and brands within this book are for clarifying purposes only and are the owned by the owners themselves, not affiliated with this document.

Table Of Contents

INTRODUCTION 1

CHAPTER 1: UNDERSTANDING THE NINJA FOODI GRILL 2

    What is the Ninja Foodi? 2

    How Does It Work? 2

    Healthier Fried Food 3

    The Benefits of Using an Electric Grill 4

    Structural Composition of the Ninja Foodi Grill 5

    How to Use the Ninja Foodi Grill 5

    Cleaning and Maintenance 7

    Troubleshooting 8

    Tips to get the most out of the Ninja Foodi 8

    FAQs 9

CHAPTER 2: BREAKFAST 11

    Savory Cauliflower Bread 11

    Pecan & Coconut Porridge 11

    French Toast 12

    Crispy Garlic Potatoes 12

    Breakfast Potatoes 13

    Egg & Turkey Sausage Cups 14

    Omelet 14

    Cheesy Broccoli Quiche 15

    Bacon Stuffed Pepper 16

    Healthy Potato Pancakes 16

    Completely Stuffed Up Bacon and Pepper 17

    Bacon & Scrambled Eggs 17

    French Toast 18

    Eggs & Veggie Burrito 19

    Breakfast Casserole 19

    Herb & Cheese Frittata 20

- French Toast Sticks 20
- Hash Browns 21
- Eggs & Avocado 22
- Pumpkin Porridge 22
- Sausage & Veggies Casserole 23

CHAPTER 3: VEGETARIAN AND VEGAN RECIPES 24
- Roasted Spicy Potatoes 24
- Grilled Cauliflower Steak 24
- Delicious Broccoli and Arugula 25
- Vegetable Fritters 26
- Crazy Fresh Onion Soup 26
- Elegant Zero Crust Kale and Mushroom Quiche 27
- Delicious Beet Borscht 27
- Pepper Jack Cauliflower Meal 28
- Slow-Cooked Brussels 28
- Honey Dressed Asparagus 29
- Italian Squash Meal 29
- Air Grilled Brussels 30
- Slowly Cooked Lemon Artichokes 30
- Well Dressed Brussels 31
- Cheddar Cauliflower Bowl 31
- A Prosciutto and Thyme Eggs 32
- The Authentic Zucchini Pesto Meal 32
- Supreme Cauliflower Soup 33
- Very Rich and Creamy Asparagus Soup 33
- Delicious Cajun Eggplant 34
- Roasted Mixed Veggies 34
- Mediterranean Veggies 35

CHAPTER 4: CHICKEN AND POULTRY RECIPES 37
- Honey & Rosemary Chicken 37
- Grilled Chicken with Veggies 37
- Excellent Chicken Tomatino 38

- Majestic Alfredo Chicken 39
- Chicken Parmesan 39
- Honey Chicken Wings 40
- Chicken Nuggets 40
- Peanut Chicken 41
- Honey Teriyaki Chicken 42
- Feisty Hot Pepper Wings Delight 42
- Grilled Garlic Chicken 43
- Grilled Balsamic Chicken Breast 43
- A Genuine Hassel Back Chicken 44
- Shredded Up Salsa Chicken 44
- Mexico's Favorite Chicken Soup 45
- Taiwanese Chicken Delight 45
- Cabbage and Chicken Meatballs 46

CHAPTER 5: FISH AND SEAFOOD RECIPES 47
- Crumbed Flounder Fillet 47
- Salmon with Coconut Aminos 47
- Lemon Garlic Shrimp 48
- Crispy Cod Fish 48
- Crispy Fish Nuggets 49
- Heartfelt Sesame Fish 49
- Awesome Sockeye Salmon 50
- Easy Fish Stew 50
- Buttery Scallops 51
- lovely Air Fried Scallops 51
- Sweet and Sour Fish 52
- Buttered Up Scallops 52
- Awesome Cherry Tomato Mackerel 53
- Lovely Air Fried Scallops 53
- Packets of Lemon and Dill Cod 54
- Adventurous Sweet and Sour Fish 54
- Garlic and Lemon Prawn Delight 55

Lovely Carb Soup 55

The Rich Guy Lobster and Butter 55

Beer-Battered Cod 56

Grilled Shrimp 57

Shrimp Boil 57

Salmon and Kale Meal 57

Lemon and Garlic Flavored Prawn Dish 58

CHAPTER 6: PORK AND OTHER RED MEAT RECIPES 60

Korean Chili Pork 60

Grilled Steak & Potatoes 60

Roast Beef with Garlic 61

Generous Pesto Beef Meal 61

Authentic Korean Flank Steak 62

Garlic Butter Pork 63

Pork with Gravy 63

Hawaiian Pork 64

Middle Eastern Lamb Stew 65

Lamb Curry 66

Deliciously Smothered Pork Chops 66

Beef and Broccoli Meal 67

Hearty New York Strip 68

Mediterranean Lamb Roast 68

Braised Lamb Shanks 69

Rosemary Lamb Chops 70

Tantalizing Beef Jerky 71

Beefed Up Spaghetti Squash 71

The Yogurt Lamb Skewers 72

Grilled Pork Chops 72

Cuban Pork Chops 73

Lettuce Cheese Steak 73

Grilled Beef Burgers 74

CHAPTER 7: DESSERT 76

- Chocolate Fudge 76
- Lime Cheesecake 76
- Baked Apples 77
- Strawberry & Cake Kebabs 77
- Mozzarella Sticks and Grilled Eggplant 78
- Almond Cherry Bars 78
- Coffee Flavored Doughnuts 79
- Ginger Cheesecake 79
- Pork Taquitos 80
- Crusted Mozzarella Sticks 80
- Simple Strawberry Cobbler 81
- Cheesy Cauliflower Steak 82
- Garlic and Mushroom Munchies 82
- Warm Glazed Up Carrots 83
- Great Mac and Cheese Bowl 83
- The Healthy Granola Bites 84
- Grilled Donuts 84
- Lemon Cheesecake 85
- Strawberry Crumble 86
- Cashew Cream 86

CONCLUSION 87

INTRODUCTION

The Ninja Foodi grill works by warming up the grill addition to a rankling 500 degrees. The hot grill plate, joined with a convection framework, courses the air and prepares food rapidly. The food falls off the grill, pleasantly seared and fresh. This arrangement of air and warmth, alongside the capacity to control cooking temperature, enables you to grill regardless of whether your food is solidified or not. That sort of accommodation is incredible for occupied families. Having the option to plunge into the cooler and grill without defrosting is a major benefit.

If the Foodi was only a grill, it would be considered as a decent kitchen appliance for families. But, the Foodi can act as an air fryer, a dehydrator, an iron, and a roaster as well. You can utilize it to prepare any way you want. However, that assignment is by all accounts for increasingly master clients. That flexibility drives the device over the line into a "must-have" category. What thrills me about cooking on the Ninja Foodi grill is that it is so cordial to kid foods. It wrenches out immaculate grilled sausages, and the iron frill can take out sure pancakes. Fly in the discretionary lack of hydration rack for some dried natural product snacks, and you have a damn child-driven kitchen cooker.

Read on to discover delicious recipes using the Ninja Foodi!

CHAPTER 1: UNDERSTANDING THE NINJA FOODI GRILL

What is the Ninja Foodi?

The Ninja Foodi Grill is a tabletop multi-function appliance that can grill, air-crisp, bake, roast, and even dehydrate.

It makes use of their cyclonic grilling technology that utilizes rapidly circulating hot air to cook seafood.

The Foodi grill is an electric grill, air fryer, convection oven, oven toaster, and dehydrator, all rolled into one

As you've probably guessed, the Ninja Foodi is not your average kitchen appliance because getting one for your home is like getting your own personal chef. The Ninja Foodi was developed through the collaboration of the Ninja engineers and a group of chefs who tested the unit at every stage of product development. The result? Even those who have no prior cooking experience can make flavor-packed meals at home that the whole family will enjoy.

The Ninja Foodi is the first to combine a pressure cooker and another very popular kitchen appliance today: the air fryer. If you look around the market, there is no shortage of kitchen gadgets that combine the slow-cooking and pressure-cooking functions. That's all well and good, but what if you want something fried and crispy? You'll have to take out either your frying pan or deep fryer to achieve the right crunch and color. This means you can make roast chicken that is juicy and tender within and beautiful bronzed and crisp outside.

How Does It Work?

The Ninja Foodi uses super-heated steam to infuse moisture into the food using the pressure-cooking function. Then, with the powerful crisping lid, the machine releases rapid-hot air down and all around the food to create the crispy finish characteristic of fried foods without having to use a lot of oil.

Each Ninja Foodi comes with the Cook & Crisp basket, which allows you to cook a 5-pound chicken, 2 pounds of chicken wings, or 3 pounds of French fries.

One of the best things about it is that it works automatically. Having a Ninja Foodi is like having a reliable kitchen assistant. For example, you forget that you were cooking something. When the cooking time is over, the Foodi automatically switches to the Keep Warm mode so your food will be the perfect temperature for when you're ready to eat.

The default duration of the Keep Warm mode is 12 hours, and you'll see the unit counting down. This way, you know how long the Ninja Foodi has been keeping your food warm at a temperature that is safe for consumption.

Additionally, it helps you plan meals ahead of time. When you know you only need one kitchen appliance to prepare everything from entree to dessert, meal planning becomes easy. And you can create a weekly schedule of meals that use mostly the same ingredients to cut back on your prep time as well as costs.

As an alternative, you can cook big batches of food during the weekend (or whenever you have free time), so you have your meals sorted throughout the week.

Another way to get a head start on your meal prep is to roast a whole chicken or make pulled pork out of a boneless pork butt. Set these aside until you are ready to add them to salads, sandwiches, and other dishes like fried rice.

Of course, the pressure-cooking function is excellent for extracting flavor from the chicken, pork, or beef bones along with vegetable scraps and make a delicious stock to be used as a soup base for noodles or pasta.

Healthier Fried Food

For many people, fried food is the best comfort food. Whether it's fried chicken, French fries, or fried street food, everyone has probably at least one fried food included on their guilty pleasure list.

Having tried it yourself, you know that frying makes your food taste delicious and crispy. However, while the flavor of foods burst in your mouth, sometimes you just can't help but think about how many calories you get from eating greasy foods.

Well, that's right, we all know how it's done. You need oil to fry, oftentimes, you need lots of it. And from what we know, too much oil on food is bad news. But did you know that it is possible to have tasty and crunchy food without having to drench your meal in oil?

Air fryers have become some of the hottest kitchen appliances today that make frying easier without the guilt. This kitchen gadget was invented to replace your traditional oil fryer with air to make it a healthy alternative to frying with oil. This innovation has been gaining a footing in many countries in the west and thus far has been making a difference in the way households prepare their food.

By definition, an air fryer is a kitchen appliance that cooks food by circulating hot air via a convection mechanism. The hot air is circulated at high speed around the food by a mechanical fan, cooking the food and making it crispy.

In America, the severe effects of obesity have been associated with the consumption of too much oily food. The use of air fryers has been gaining praise due to its promising offer as a beneficial solution to the long-existing problem of obesity as a result of eating oil-filled food. Its auspicious contribution in making a healthier lifestyle through healthy eating is what makes these types of gizmos very appealing, especially to those who are trying to lose weight and those who are aiming for healthier living.

When it comes to modern-day cooking, one of the coolest gadgets that you can own in your household is an air fryer that does it all—a real ninja in the kitchen.

Ninja is one big name in the kitchen gadget. While it is best known for its blenders, this company is one of the best makers of the best air fryers in the market. With its sleek black design and high functionality of its air fryers, every unit looks great in any kitchen.

If you have been contemplating on whether an air fryer is worth the purchase, you may want to know what it does for you. At fingertips, you can have an appliance that can imitate foods made in oil fryers, only that it is healthier and guilt-free with Ninja Air Fryer Max XL. This air fryer will serve up many ways of making life more comfortable—a wise choice for every household.

For those who can't live without fried food, using an air fryer is an excellent choice to cut down fat and calories from your food. Less oil means fewer calories.

The Benefits of Using an Electric Grill

Whether it is a trend or the general convenience of it, more people are appreciating smaller and more portable indoor cookers due to a number of benefits from owning one.

Compact

Electric grills are small enough to fit on most kitchen counters and tables. It is also portable enough to be easily transported or moved around.

Smokeless

This is probably one of the best things about indoor electric grills. People who do not have any access to open areas can still enjoy grilling since it does not produce smoke like standard grillers.

Multi-function

Most indoor cookers come with various functionalities giving you more value for your money. It can also eliminate the need to purchase other appliances and save you essential kitchen space.

Easy to clean and operate

Indoor grills are plug-and-play appliances making them user-friendly to a wider demographic. The cooking components are coated with a non-stick ceramic material that can be effortlessly taken apart and cleaned using a standard dishwasher.

Grill marks

Like traditional outdoor grills, indoor grills can also give meat and other foods those appetizing grill marks. Although, the Ninja Foodi's grill marks are curved, unlike the typical straight markings you get from regular outdoor grills.

Browns and crisps food

Indoor grills like the Ninja Foodi use circulating hot air to cook the food thoroughly. This creates delectable flavors through a browning process called the Maillard reaction. Similar to convection ovens and toasters, the Ninja Foodi is excellent at making food crunchy when you need it to be.

Capable of high temperatures

A wide range of temperature settings let you cook a variety of foods from char-grilled vegetables to restaurant-level steaks. Unlike other tabletop cookers, the Ninja Grill will let you cook frozen foods without the need to defrost them. It can also get as hot as 500-510 degrees Fahrenheit.

Structural Composition of the Ninja Foodi Grill

Although the Ninja Foodi is a countertop cooker, it does come in a hefty size. But given its multi-purpose functionality and convenience over conventional single-purpose appliances, the size can easily be excused.

The hood houses the heating element and the convection fans that help sear meat and eliminate the need to flip food. The grill grates, crisper basket, and cooking pot are all coated with a non-stick ceramic finish.

All cooking components are safe to use as it is manufactured without harmful chemicals such as PTFE, PFOA, and BPA.

A grease collector at the back prevents any spillage and makes cleaning a breeze. The kebab skewers and roasting rack are all made of food-safe stainless steel as well.

The power cable is three meters long and is intended to keep the grill close to an outlet and prevent people from tripping over lengthy cords.

How to Use the Ninja Foodi Grill

When you are cooking for the first time with your Foodi grill, you must first wash the detachable cooking parts with warm soapy water to remove any oil and debris. Let them air dry, and place them back inside once you are ready to cook. An easy-to-follow instruction guide comes with each unit, so make sure to go over it prior to cooking.

Position your grill on a level and secure surface. Leave at least 6 inches of space around it, especially at the back where the air intake vent and air socket are located. Ensure that the splatter guard is installed whenever the grill is in use. This is a wire mesh that covers the heating element on the inside of the lid.

For grilling

Plug your unit into an outlet and power on the grill.

Use the grill grate over the cooking pot and choose the grill function. This has four default temperature settings of low at 400°F, medium at 450°F, high at 500°F, and max at 510°F.

Set the time needed to cook. You may check the grilling cheat sheet that comes with your unit to guide you with the time and temperature settings. It is best to check the food regularly depending on the doneness you prefer and to avoid overcooking.

Once the required settings are selected, press start and wait for the digital display to show 'add food.' The unit will start to preheat similar to an oven and will show the progress through the display. This step takes about 8 minutes.

If you need to check the food or flip it, the timer will pause and resume once the lid is closed.

The screen will show 'Done' once the cooking is complete. Power off the unit and unplug the device. Leave the hood open to let the unit cool faster.

For roasting

Remove the grill grates and use the cooking pot that comes with the unit. You may also purchase their roasting rack for this purpose.

Press the roast option and set the timer between 1 to 4 hours depending on the recipe requirements. The Foodi will preheat for 3 minutes regardless of the time you have set.

Once ready, place the meat directly on the roasting pot or rack.

Check occasionally for doneness. A meat thermometer is another useful tool to get your meats perfectly cooked.

For baking

Remove the grates and use the cooking pot.

Choose the bake setting and set your preferred temperature and time. Preheating will take about 3 minutes.

Once done with preheating, you may put the ingredients directly on the cooking pot, or you may use your regular baking tray. An 8-inch baking tray can fit inside as well as similar-sized oven-safe containers.

For air frying/air crisping

Put the crisper basket in and close the lid.

Press the Air Crisp or Air Fry option then the Start button. The default temperature is set at 390°F and will preheat at about 3 minutes. You can adjust the temperature and time by pressing the buttons beside these options.

If you do not need to preheat, just press the **Air Crisp** button a second time and the display will show you the 'add food' message.

Put the food inside and shake or turn every 10 minutes. Use oven mitts or tongs with silicone tips when doing this.

For dehydrating

Place the first layer of food directly on the cooking pot.

Add the crisper basket and add one more layer.

Choose the Dehydrate setting and set the timer between 7 to 10 hours.

You may check the progress from time to time.

For cooking frozen foods

Choose the medium heat, which is 450°F using the grill option. You may also use the Air Crisp option if you are cooking fries, vegetables, and other frozen foods.

Set the time needed for your recipe. Add a few minutes to compensate for the thawing.

Flip or shake after a few minutes to cook the food evenly.

Cleaning and Maintenance

The components are dishwasher-safe and are fabricated with a non-stick ceramic coating, to make clean-up and maintenance easier. Plus, the grill conveniently comes with a plastic cleaning brush with a scraper at the other end.

Cleaning tips

Let the grill cool down completely and ensure that it is unplugged from the power outlet before trying to clean the unit.

Take out the splatter guard, grill grates, and cooking pot, and soak them in soapy water for a few hours to let the debris soften and make cleaning easier. Wash only the removable parts.

Gently brush off dirt and debris using the plastic brush that comes with your grill. Use the other end of the brush to dislodge food in hard to reach areas.

Let the parts dry thoroughly.

Clean the insides and exterior of the unit with a clean damp cloth.

Maintenance tips

Always keep your unit clean, especially before putting in a new batch for cooking. You should clean the parts and the unit after each use.

Never use cleaning instruments or chemicals that are too harsh and can damage the coating.

Keep the electrical cords away from children and any traffic in your kitchen.

Avoid getting the unit and electrical components wet and place it away from areas that constantly get soaked or damp.

Always unplug the unit when not in use.

Troubleshooting

Smoke coming out of the grill

Although the Ninja Foodi is virtually smokeless as advertised, you may see some smoke from time to time for a number of reasons.

One is the type of oil you use for cooking. Ideally, canola, grapeseed, and avocado oil should be used since they have a high smoke point. This means that they do not produce smoke or burn at high temperatures. Other oils with high smoke points include corn, almond, safflower, sesame, and sunflower oils.

Another reason is the accumulation of grease at the bottom of the pot. If you continuously cook foods that produce a lot of grease and oil, this will burn and create smoke. Empty and clean the pot before cooking the next batch.

The grill is showing 'Add Food'

This means that the unit has finished preheating and that you can now put food inside the grill.

The control panel is shows 'Shut Lid'

Try opening the lid and closing it securely until the message is gone.

Unit is unresponsive and only shows 'E' on the panel

Your unit is damaged, and you need to contact customer service.

Tips to get the most out of the Ninja Foodi

Here are some useful tips you can use when cooking with the Ninja Foodi as well as some commonly asked questions to guide you if you are planning to purchase one for yourself.

Brush or spray the grates with some canola oil, corn oil, or avocado oil to avoid smoke.

A light coating of oil will make your air-fried French fries taste better.

Use the time charts as a guide, but make sure you check the food regularly since the grill gets hot and can cook quickly. You may also use a meat thermometer in your food to cook exactly the way you want.

Use silicone or wooden utensils. Never stick metal tongs or cutleries on your grill to avoid electric shock and damaging the ceramic coating.

If you are planning to do a lot of dehydrating and baking, it will be helpful to purchase their food rack and baking pan.

If the timer was up but you need to cook the food longer, simply adjust the timer and press the start button to continue cooking.

Although preheating is recommended to get the finest results, you can skip this step by pressing the option a second time.

To get juicier meat, let it rest at least 5 minutes before slicing.

FAQs

Is it worth the price?

If you are getting the Foodi grill as a secondary appliance, it may seem pricey. But given the various functions, you are getting with one equipment, the value for money will be apparent with continuous use.

Can it heat up the kitchen as most ovens do?

No. One great thing about portable cookers like the Ninja Foodi grill is that it does not make the kitchen uncomfortably hot, making it ideal for use even during the summer.

What button should I press to pause the timer?

Opening the lid will automatically pause the timer.

Why my food is not evenly cooked when air fried?

It is best not to overcrowd food inside the crisper basket. Create an even layer to get better results. You need to flip or shake the food every few minutes to have even browning.

How do I convert cooking temperatures from recipes meant for regular ovens?

You can simply reduce the temperature required by 25 degrees Fahrenheit when using the Ninja Foodi grill. You will have to check the food regularly to make sure it is not overcooked.

Chapter 2: Breakfast

Savory Cauliflower Bread

Preparation time: 15 minutes

Cooking time: 4 hours Servings: 8

INGREDIENTS:

12 ounces cauliflower florets

2 large organic eggs

2 cups mozzarella cheese, shredded and divided

3 tablespoons coconut flour

Salt and ground black pepper, as required

2 garlic cloves, minced

DIRECTIONS:

In a food processor, include cauliflower and heartbeat until a rice-like consistency is achieved.

Transfer the cauliflower rice into a large bowl.

Add 1 cup of the cheese, eggs, coconut flour, salt, and black pepper, and mix until well combined.

In the greased pot of the Ninja Foodi, place the cauliflower mixture and press firmly.

Sprinkle with garlic and remaining cheese evenly.

Close the Ninja Foodi with the crisping lid and select **Slow Cooker**.

Set on **High** for 2-4 hours.

Press **Start/Stop** to begin cooking.

Keep the bread inside for about 5-10 minutes.

Carefully, remove the bread from the pot and place onto a platter.

Cut the bread into desired-sized slices and serve warm.

NUTRITIONAL:

Calories: 72

Fats: 3.3 g

Net Carbs: 2.9 g

Carbs: 5.9 g

Fiber: 3 g

Sugar: 1.5 g

Proteins: 5.2 g

Sodium: 104 mg

Pecan & Coconut Porridge

Preparation time: 15 minutes

Cooking time: 1 hour

Servings: 4

INGREDIENTS:

1 cup pecan halves

½ cup unsweetened dried coconut shreds

¼ cup pumpkin seeds, shelled

1 cup water

2 teaspoons butter, melted

4-6 drops liquid Stevia

DIRECTIONS:

In a food processor, add the walnuts, coconut, and pumpkin seeds, and pulse for about 30 seconds.

In the pot of the Ninja Foodi, place the pecan mixture and remaining ingredients, and stir to combine.

Close the Ninja Foodi with the crisping lid and select **Slow Cooker**.

Set on **High** for 1 hour.

Press **Start/Stop** to begin cooking.

Serve warm.

NUTRITIONAL:

Calories: 317

Fats: 31.5 g

Net Carbs: 2.9 g

Carbs: 7.5 g

Fiber: 4.6 g

Sugar: 1.8 g

Proteins: 5.8 g

Sodium: 19 mg

French Toast

Preparation Time: 15 minutes

Cooking Time: 10 minutes

Servings: 4

INGREDIENTS:

6 eggs

1 cup milk

1 cup heavy cream

1 teaspoon honey

Cooking spray

1 loaf French bread, sliced

½ cup butter

½ cup sugar

DIRECTIONS:

Beat the eggs in a bowl.

Stir in milk, cream, and honey.

Dip the bread slices into the mixture.

Add to the grill basket inside the Ninja Foodi Grill.

Spread some butter and sprinkle sugar on top of the bread slices.

Seal the pot and air fry at 350°F for 5-10 minutes.

Serving Suggestions

Serve with maple syrup.

Preparation/Cooking Tips

It's a good idea to use day-old bread for this recipe.

NUTRITIONAL:

Calories: 72

Fats: 3.3 g

Net Carbs: 2.9 g

Carbs: 5.9 g

Fiber: 3 g

Sugar: 1.5 g

Proteins: 5.2 g

Sodium: 104 mg

Crispy Garlic Potatoes

Preparation Time: 10 minutes

Cooking Time: 20 minutes

Servings: 8

INGREDIENTS:

1½ lb. potatoes, diced

1 tablespoon avocado oil

1 teaspoon garlic powder

Salt and pepper to taste

DIRECTIONS:

Toss the potatoes in oil.

Season with garlic powder, salt, and pepper.

Add the air fryer basket to the Ninja Foodi Grill.

Select the Air Fry setting.

Cook at 400°F for 20 minutes, tossing halfway through.

Serving Suggestions

Sprinkle with chopped turkey bacon crisps.

Preparation/Cooking Tips

You can also season the potatoes with paprika.

NUTRITIONAL:

Calories: 70

Fats: 3 g

Net Carbs: 2 g

Carbs: 5 g

Fiber: 3 g

Sugar: 1 g

Proteins: 5 g

Sodium: 100 mg

Breakfast Potatoes

Preparation Time: 10 minutes

Cooking Time: 20 minutes

Servings: 8

INGREDIENTS:

2 potatoes, scrubbed, rinsed, and diced

1 tablespoon olive oil

Salt to taste

¼ teaspoon garlic powder

DIRECTIONS:

Put the potatoes in a bowl of cold water. Soak for 45 minutes.

Pat the potatoes dry with a paper towel. Toss in olive oil, salt, and garlic powder.

Put in the Ninja Foodi basket. Seal the crisping lid. Set it to **Air Crisp**.

Cook at 400°F for 20 minutes. Flip the potatoes halfway through.

Serving Suggestion: Garnish with chopped parsley.

Tips: Cook the potatoes on a single layer. Do not overcrowd.

Nutritional Information (Per Serving):

Calories: 208

Total Fat: 7.2 g

Saturated Fat: 1.1 g

Cholesterol: 0 mg

Sodium: 90 mg

Total Carbohydrate: 33.7 g

Dietary Fiber: 5.1 g

Total Sugars: 2.5 g

Protein: 3.6 g

Potassium: 871 mg

Egg & Turkey Sausage Cups

Preparation Time: 10 minutes

Cooking Time: 30 minutes

Servings: 8

INGREDIENTS:

8 tablespoons turkey sausage, cooked and crumbled, divided

8 tablespoons frozen spinach, chopped and divided

8 teaspoons shredded cheddar cheese, divided

4 eggs

DIRECTIONS:

Add a layer of the sausage, spinach, and cheese to each muffin cup.

Crack the egg open on top. Seal the crisping lid. Set it to **Air Crisp**.

Cook at 330°F for 10 minutes.

Serving Suggestion: Sprinkle basil and Parmesan on top.

Tips:

You can also use Monterey Jack cheese in place of the cheddar.

Nutritional Information (Per Serving):

Calories: 171

Total Fat: 13.3 g

Saturated Fat: 4.7 g

Cholesterol: 190 mg

Sodium: 289 mg

Total Carbohydrate: 0.5 g

Dietary Fiber: 0.1 g

Total Sugars: 0.4 g

Protein: 11.9 g

Potassium: 161 mg

Omelet

Preparation Time: 10 minutes

Cooking Time: 40 minutes

Servings: 8

INGREDIENTS:

2 eggs

¼ cup milk

1 tablespoon red bell pepper, chopped

1 slice ham, diced

1 tablespoon mushroom, chopped

Salt to taste

¼ cup cheese, shredded

DIRECTIONS:

Whisk the eggs and milk in a bowl. Add the ham and vegetables. Season with the salt.

Pour the mixture into a small pan. Place the pan inside the Ninja Foodi basket.

Seal the crisping lid. Set it to **Air Crisp**. Cook at 350°F for 8 minutes.

Before it is fully cooked, sprinkle the cheese on top.

Coat the beef cubes with the salt and pickling spice.

In a skillet over medium heat, pour in the olive oil.

Serving Suggestion

Garnish with chopped green onion.

Tips:

Use a combination of cheddar and Mozzarella.

Nutritional Information (Per Serving):

Calories: 177

Total Fat: 11 g

Saturated Fat: 5.1 g

Cholesterol: 189 mg

Sodium: 425 mg

Total Carbohydrate: 7.1 g

Dietary Fiber: 1 g

Total Sugars: 4.8 g

Protein: 13.1 g

Potassium: 249 mg

Cheesy Broccoli Quiche

Preparation Time: 10 minutes

Cooking Time: 40 minutes

Servings: 8

INGREDIENTS:

1 cup water

2 cups broccoli florets

1 carrot, chopped

1 cup cheddar cheese, grated

¼ cup Feta cheese, crumbled

¼ cup milk

2 eggs

1 teaspoon parsley

1 teaspoon thyme

Salt and pepper to taste

DIRECTIONS:

Pour the water inside the Ninja Foodi. Place the basket inside.

Put the carrots and broccoli on the basket. Cover the pot.

Set it to pressure. Cook at high pressure for 2 minutes.

Release the pressure quickly. Crack the eggs into a bowl and beat.

Season with the salt, pepper, parsley, and thyme. Put the vegetables on a small baking pan. Layer with the cheese and pour in the beaten eggs. Place on the basket.

Choose the Air Crisp function. Seal the crisping lid. Cook at 350°F for 20 minutes.

Serving Suggestion:

Garnish with chopped parsley or chives.

Tips:

Try other types of cheese for this recipe.

Nutritional Information Per Serving:

Calories: 401

Total Fat: 28 g

Saturated Fat: 16.5 g

Cholesterol: 242 mg

Sodium: 688 mg

Total Carbohydrate: 12.8 g

Dietary Fiber: 3.3 g

Total Sugars: 5.8 g

Protein: 26.2 g

Potassium: 537 mg

Bacon Stuffed Pepper

Preparation Time: 10 minutes

Cooking Time: 15 minutes

Servings: 4

INGREDIENTS:

4 slices bacon, cooked and chopped

4 large eggs

1 cup cheddar cheese, shredded

4 bell peppers, seeded and tops removed

Salt and pepper to taste

Chopped parsley, for garnish

DIRECTIONS:

Take your bell peppers and divide cheese and bacon between them.

Crack an egg into each of the bell peppers. Season them with salt and pepper.

Preheat your Ninja Foodi by pressing the Air Crisp option and setting it to 390°F.

Set your timer to 15 minutes.

Allow it to preheat until it beeps.

Transfer bell pepper to your cooking basket and transfer to Foodi Grill.

Lock the lid and cook for 10-15 minutes until egg whites are cooked well until the yolks are slightly runny.

Remove peppers from the basket and garnish with parsley.

Serve and enjoy!

Nutritional Values (Per Serving)

Calories: 326

Fat: 23 g

Saturated Fat: 10 g

Carbohydrates: 10 g

Fiber: 2 g

Sodium: 781 mg

Protein: 22 g

Healthy Potato Pancakes

Preparation Time: 10 minutes

Cooking Time: 24 minutes

Servings: 4

INGREDIENTS:

Salt and pepper to taste

3 tablespoons flour

¼ teaspoon salt

½ teaspoon garlic powder

2 tablespoons unsalted butter

¼ cup milk

1 egg, beaten

1 medium onion, chopped

4 medium potatoes, peeled and cleaned

DIRECTIONS:

Take your potatoes and peel them. Shred the potatoes and soak the shredded potatoes under cold water.

Drain your potatoes in a colander.

In a separate bowl, add milk, eggs, butter, garlic powder, pepper, and salt. Add flour and mix the whole mixture well.

Add shredded potatoes.

Preheat your Ninja Foodi to Air Crisp mode with a temperature of 390°F, setting the timer to 24 minutes.

Once you hear the beep, add ¼ cup of potato pancake batter to the cooking basket.

Cook for 12 minutes until you have a nice golden texture.

Repeat with remaining batter.

Serve once done, enjoy!

Nutritional Values (Per Serving)

Calories: 240

Fat: 11 g

Saturated Fat: 3 g

Carbohydrates: 33 g

Fiber: 4 g

Sodium: 259 mg

Protein: 6 g

Completely Stuffed Up Bacon and Pepper

Preparation Time: 10 minutes

Cooking Time: 15 minutes

Servings: 4

INGREDIENTS:

Chopped parsley, for garnish

Salt and pepper to taste

4 whole large eggs

4 bell pepper, seeded and tops removed

4 slices bacon, cooked and chopped

1 cup cheddar cheese, shredded

DIRECTIONS:

Take the bell pepper and divide the cheese and bacon evenly between them.

Crack eggs into each of the bell pepper.

Season the bell pepper with salt and pepper.

Preheat your Ninja Food Grill in Air Crisp mode with temperature to 390°F.

Set timer to 15 minutes.

Once you hear the beep, transfer the bell pepper to the cooking basket.

Transfer your prepared pepper to Ninja Foodi Grill and cook for 10-15 minutes until the eggs are cooked, and the yolks are just slightly runny.

Garnish with a bit of parsley.

Enjoy!

Nutritional Values (Per Serving)

Calories: 326

Fat: 23 g

Saturated Fat: 10 g

Carbohydrates: 10 g

Fiber: 2 g

Sodium: 781 mg

Protein: 22 g

Bacon & Scrambled Eggs

Preparation Time: 10 minutes

Cooking Time: 25 minutes

Servings: 4

INGREDIENTS:

4 strips bacon

2 eggs

1 tablespoon milk

Salt and pepper to taste

DIRECTIONS:

Place the bacon inside the Ninja Foodi. Set it to **Air Crisp**.

Cover the crisping lid. Cook at 390°F for 3 minutes.

Flip the bacon and cook for another 2 minutes. Remove the bacon and set aside.

Whisk the eggs and milk in a bowl. Season with the salt and pepper.

Set the Ninja Foodi to **Sauté**. Add the eggs and cook until firm.

Serving Suggestion:

Serve with toasted bread.

Tips:

You can add herbs to the egg.

Nutritional Information Per Serving:

Calories: 272

Total Fat: 20.4 g

Saturated Fat: 6.7 g

Cholesterol: 206 mg

Sodium: 943 mg

Total Carbohydrate: 1.3 g

Dietary Fiber: 0 g

Total Sugars: 0.7 g

Protein: 19.9 g

Potassium: 279 mg

French Toast

Preparation Time: 10 minutes

Cooking Time: 35 minutes

Servings: 4

INGREDIENTS:

2 eggs, beaten

¼ cup milk

¼ cup brown sugar

1 tablespoon honey

1 teaspoon cinnamon

¼ teaspoon nutmeg

4 slices wholemeal bread, sliced into strips

DIRECTIONS:

In a bowl, combine all the ingredients except the bread. Mix well.

Dip each strip in the mixture. Place the bread strips in the Ninja Foodi basket.

Place basket inside the pot. Cover with the crisping lid. Set it to **Air Crisp**.

Cook at 320°F for 10 minutes.

Serving Suggestion:

Dust with confectioners' sugar.

Tips:

You can also add berries or serve with oatmeal.

Nutritional Information Per Serving:

Calories: 295

Total Fat: 6.1 g

Saturated Fat: 2.1 g

Cholesterol: 166 mg

Sodium: 332 mg

Total Carbohydrate: 49.8 g

Dietary Fiber: 3.9 g

Total Sugars: 29.4 g

Protein: 11.9 g

Potassium: 112 mg

Eggs & Veggie Burrito

Preparation Time: 10 minutes

Cooking Time: 25 minutes

Servings: 4

INGREDIENTS:

3 eggs, beaten

Salt and pepper to taste

Cooking spray

8 tortillas

2 red bell peppers, sliced into strips

1 onion, sliced thinly

DIRECTIONS:

Beat the eggs in a bowl. Season with the salt and pepper. Set aside.

Choose the Sauté mode in the Ninja Foodi. Spray with the oil. Cook the vegetables until soft. Remove and set aside. Pour in the eggs to the pot. Cook until firm.

Wrap the eggs and veggies with a tortilla.

Serving Suggestion

Sprinkle top part with cheese.

Tips:

You can also add carrot sticks to this recipe.

Nutritional Information Per Serving:

Calories: 92

Total Fat: 2.5 g

Saturated Fat: 0.6 g

Cholesterol: 61 mg

Sodium: 35 mg

Total Carbohydrate: 14.4 g

Dietary Fiber: 2.2 g

Total Sugars: 2.4 g

Protein: 3.9 g

Potassium: 143 mg

Breakfast Casserole

Preparation Time: 10 minutes

Cooking Time: 30 minutes

Servings: 4

INGREDIENTS:

Cooking spray

1 lb. hash brown

1 lb. breakfast sausage, cooked and crumbled

1 red bell pepper, diced

1 green bell pepper, diced

1 onion, diced

4 eggs

Salt and pepper to taste

DIRECTIONS:

Coat a small baking pan with oil. Place the hash browns on the bottom part.

Add the sausage, and then the onion and bell peppers.

Place the pan on top of the Ninja Foodi basket. Put the basket inside the pot.

Close the crisping lid. Set it to Air Crisp. Cook at 350°F for 10 minutes.

Open the lid. Crack the eggs on top. Cook for another 10 minutes.

Season with the salt and pepper.

Serving Suggestion:

Garnish with fresh basil leaves.

Tips:

Use yellow onion for this recipe.

Nutritional Information (Per Serving):

Calories: 513

Total Fat: 34 g

Saturated Fat: 9.3 g

Cholesterol: 173 mg

Sodium: 867 mg

Total Carbohydrate: 30 g

Dietary Fiber: 3.1 g

Total Sugars: 3.1 g

Protein: 21.1 g

Potassium: 761 mg

Herb & Cheese Frittata

Preparation Time: 10 minutes

Cooking Time: 25 minutes

Servings: 4

INGREDIENTS:

4 eggs

½ cup half and half

2 tablespoons parsley, chopped

2 tablespoons chives, chopped

¼ cup shredded cheddar cheese

Salt and pepper to taste

DIRECTIONS:

Beat the eggs in a bowl. Add the rest of the ingredients and stir well.

Pour the mixture into a small baking pan.

Place the pan on top of the Ninja Foodi basket.

Seal the crisping lid. Set it to **Air Crisp**. Cook at 330°F for 15 minutes.

Serving Suggestion:

Garnish with fresh cilantro.

Tips:

Insert a toothpick into the frittata. If the toothpick comes out clean, it means it is already fully cooked.

Nutritional Information Per Serving:

Calories: 132

Total Fat: 10.2 g

Saturated Fat: 5 g

Cholesterol: 182 mg

Sodium: 119 mg

Total Carbohydrate: 1. 9g

Dietary Fiber: 0.1 g

Total Sugars: 0.5 g

Protein: 8.3 g

Potassium: 121 mg

French Toast Sticks

Preparation Time: 10 minutes

Cooking Time: 10 minutes

Servings: 12

INGREDIENTS:

5 eggs

1 cup almond milk

¼ cup sugar

1 teaspoon vanilla extract

4 tablespoons melted butter

4 bread slices, sliced into 12 sticks

DIRECTIONS:

Beat the eggs in a bowl.

Stir in milk, sugar, vanilla, and butter.

Dip the breadsticks into the mixture.

Add these to the air fryer basket and place inside the Ninja Foodi Grill.

Air fry at 350°F for 8-10 minutes.

Serving Suggestions:

Sprinkle with cinnamon powder before serving.

Preparation/Cooking Tips:

Prepare in advance and freeze for later use.

Nutritional Values (Per Serving)

Calories: 120

Fat: 10 g

Saturated Fat: 2 g

Carbohydrates: 30 g

Fiber: 5 g

Sodium: 149 mg

Protein: 3 g

Hash Browns

Preparation Time: 15 minutes

Cooking Time: 20 minutes

Servings: 4

INGREDIENTS:

6 potatoes, grated

1 onion, chopped

1 bell pepper, chopped

2 teaspoons olive oil

Salt and pepper to taste

DIRECTIONS:

Toss the grated potatoes, onion, and bell pepper separately in oil.

Season with salt and pepper.

Add potatoes to the air fryer.

Air fry at 400°F for 10 minutes.

Shake and stir in onion and pepper.

Cook for another 10 minutes.

Serving Suggestions:

Serve with a side salad.

Preparation/Cooking Tips:

Soak the potatoes in water for 30 minutes after grating. Dry completely with paper towels before cooking. This technique results in a crispier hash brown.

Nutritional Values (Per Serving)

Calories: 240

Fat: 11 g

Saturated Fat: 3 g

Carbohydrates: 33 g

Fiber: 4 g

Sodium: 259 mg

Protein: 6 g

Eggs & Avocado

Preparation Time: 10 minutes

Cooking Time: 15 minutes

Servings: 2

INGREDIENTS:

1 avocado, sliced in half and pitted

2 eggs

Salt and pepper to taste

Cheddar cheese, shredded

DIRECTIONS:

Scoop out about a tablespoon of avocado flesh to make a hole.

Crack the egg on top of the avocado.

Season with salt and pepper.

Sprinkle with cheese.

Air fry at 390°F for 12 to 15 minutes.

Serving Suggestion

Serve with salsa or hot sauce.

Preparation/Cooking Tips

Scoop out more avocado flesh to create a bigger hole for the egg.

Nutritional Values (Per Serving)

Calories: 200

Fat: 19 g

Saturated Fat: 5 g

Carbohydrates: 23 g

Fiber: 5 g

Sodium: 159 mg

Protein: 9 g

Pumpkin Porridge

Preparation time: 15 minutes

Cooking time: 5 hours

Servings: 8

INGREDIENTS:

1 cup unsweetened almond milk, divided

2 pounds pumpkin, peeled and cubed into ½-inch pieces

6-8 drops liquid Stevia

½ teaspoon ground allspice

1 tablespoon ground cinnamon

1 teaspoon ground nutmeg

¼ teaspoon ground cloves

DIRECTIONS:

In the pot of Ninja Foodi, place ½ cup of almond milk and remaining ingredients and stir to combine.

Close the Ninja Foodi with the crisping lid and select **Slow Cooker**.

Set on **Low** for 4-5 hours.

Press **Start/Stop** to begin cooking.

Stir in the remaining almond milk and with a potato masher, mash the mixture completely.

Serve warm.

NUTRITIONAL:

Calories: 48

Fats: 0.9 g

Net Carbs: 6 g

Carbs: 10 g

Fiber: 4 g

Sugar: 3.8 g

Proteins: 1.4 g

Sodium: 29 mg

Sausage & Veggies Casserole

Preparation time: 15 minutes

Cooking time: 7 hours 3 minutes

Servings: 8

INGREDIENTS:

2½ cups cauliflower florets

12 organic eggs

¾ cup unsweetened almond milk

1 teaspoon dried oregano, crushed

¾ teaspoon paprika

Salt, as required

1 red ringer pepper, seeded and cleaved finely

1 lb. gluten-free cooked sausages, cut into slices

1½ cups cheddar cheese, grated

DIRECTIONS:

In an enormous pot of bubbling water, cook cauliflower for about 2-3 minutes.

Expel from the warmth and channel the cauliflower completely. Set aside to cool.

In a bowl, add the eggs, almond milk, and oregano, paprika, and salt and beat until well combined.

In the greased pot of the Ninja Foodi, place the cauliflower followed by the bell pepper, sausage slices, and cheddar cheese.

Top with the egg mixture evenly.

Close the Ninja Foodi with the crisping lid and select **Slow Cooker**.

Set on **Low** for 6-7 hours.

Press **Start/Stop** to begin cooking.

Cut into equal-sized wedges and serve hot.

Nutritional:

Calories: 389

Fats: 30.1 g

Net Carbs: 2.8 g

Carbs: 4 g

Fiber: 1.2 g

Sugar: 2.2 g

Proteins: 25.2 g

Sodium: 695 mg

Chapter 3: Vegetarian and Vegan Recipes

Roasted Spicy Potatoes

Preparation Time: 15 minutes

Cooking Time: 25 minutes

Servings: 4

INGREDIENTS:

1 lb. baby potatoes, sliced into wedges

2 tablespoons olive oil

Salt to taste

1 tablespoon garlic powder

1 tablespoon paprika

½ cup mayonnaise

2 tablespoons white wine vinegar

2 tablespoons tomato paste

1 teaspoon chili powder

DIRECTIONS:

Toss potatoes in oil.

Sprinkle with salt, garlic powder, and paprika.

Add crisper plate to the air fryer basket.

Add a basket to the Ninja Foodi Grill.

Set it to **Air Fry**. Set it to 360°F for 30 minutes.

Press **Start** to preheat.

Put the potatoes on the crisper plate after 3 minutes.

Cook for 25 minutes.

While waiting, mix the remaining ingredients.

Toss potatoes in spicy mayo mixture and serve.

Serving Suggestions:

Sprinkle with chopped parsley before serving.

Preparation/Cooking Tips:

Poke potatoes with a fork before roasting.

Nutritional Values (Per Serving)

Calories: 178

Fat: 10 g

Saturated Fat: 5 g

Carbohydrates: 39 g

Fiber: 6 g

Sodium: 29 mg

Protein: 5 g

Grilled Cauliflower Steak

Preparation Time: 30 minutes

Cooking Time: 25 minutes

Servings: 2

INGREDIENTS:

2 cauliflower steaks

¼ cup vegetable oil, divided

Salt and pepper to taste

1 onion, chopped

3 cloves garlic, minced

½ cup roasted red bell peppers, chopped

¼ cup Kalamata olives, chopped

1 tablespoon fresh parsley, chopped

1 tablespoon fresh oregano, chopped

½ lb. feta cheese, crumbled

1 tablespoon lemon juice

1/4 cup walnuts, chopped

DIRECTIONS:

Add grill grate to your Ninja Foodi Grill.

Choose the Grill setting.

Set it to **Max** for 17 minutes.

Press **Start** to preheat.

Brush both sides of cauliflower steaks with oil.

Season with salt and pepper.

Grill for 10 minutes per side.

Mix the remaining ingredients in a bowl.

Spread mixture on top of the steaks and cook for another 2 minutes.

Serving Suggestions:

Serve as a vegetarian main dish.

Preparation/Cooking Tips:

Use ricotta cheese in place of feta if not available.

Nutritional Values (Per Serving)

Calories: 240

Fat: 11 g

Saturated Fat: 3 g

Carbohydrates: 33 g

Fiber: 4 g

Sodium: 259 mg

Protein: 6 g

Delicious Broccoli and Arugula

Preparation Time: 10 minutes

Cooking Time: 12 minutes

Servings: 4

INGREDIENTS:

Pepper as needed

½ teaspoon salt

Red pepper flakes

2 tablespoons extra virgin olive oil

1 tablespoon canola oil

½ red onion, sliced

1 garlic cloves, minced

1 teaspoon Dijon mustard

1 teaspoon honey

1 tablespoon lemon juice

2 tablespoons parmesan cheese, grated

4 cups arugula, torn

2 heads broccoli, trimmed

DIRECTIONS:

Preheat your Ninja Foodi Grill to **Max** and set the timer to 12 minutes.

Take a large-sized bowl and add broccoli, sliced onion, and canola oil, toss the mixture well until coated.

Once you hear the beep, it is preheated.

Arrange your vegetables over the grill grate, let them grill for 8-12 minutes.

Take a medium-sized bowl and whisk in lemon juice, olive oil, mustard, honey, garlic, red pepper flakes, pepper, and salt.

Once done, add the prepared veggies and arugula to a bowl.

Drizzle the prepared vinaigrette on top, sprinkle a bit of parmesan.

Stir and mix.

Enjoy!

Nutritional Values (Per Serving)

Calories: 168

Fat: 12 g

Saturated Fat: 3 g

Carbohydrates: 13 g

Fiber: 1 g

Sodium: 392 mg

Protein: 6 g

Vegetable Fritters

Preparation Time: 10 minutes

Cooking Time: 40 minutes

Servings: 4

3 tablespoons ground flaxseed mixed with 1/2 cup water

2 potatoes, shredded

2 cups frozen mixed vegetables

1 cup frozen peas, thawed

½ cup onion, chopped

¼ cup fresh cilantro, chopped

½ cup almond flour

Salt to taste

Cooking spray

DIRECTIONS:

Combine all the ingredients in a bowl. Form patties. Spray each patty with oil.

Transfer to the Ninja Foodi basket. Set it to **Air Crisp**. Close the crisping lid.

Cook at 360°F for 15 minutes, flipping halfway through.

Tips:

You can also omit the cooking spray for an oil-free recipe.

Nutritional Information Per Serving:

Calories: 171

Total Fat: 0.5 g

Saturated Fat: 0.1 g

Cholesterol: 0 mg

Sodium: 107 mg

Total Carbohydrate: 35.7 g

Dietary Fiber: 9.1 g

Total Sugars: 6.5 g

Iron: 2 mg

Crazy Fresh Onion Soup

Preparation time: 5 minutes

Cooking time: 10-15 minutes

Servings: 3

INGREDIENTS:

2 tablespoons avocado oil

8 cups yellow onion

1 tablespoon balsamic vinegar

6 cups of pork stock

1 teaspoon salt

2 bay leaves

2 large sprigs, fresh thyme

DIRECTIONS:

Cut up the onion in half through the root.

Peel them and slice into thin half-moons.

Set the pot to Sauté mode and add oil. Once the oil is hot, add the onions.

Cook for about 15 minutes.

Add balsamic vinegar and scrape any fond from the bottom.

Add stock, bay leaves, salt, and thyme.

Lock up the lid and cook on high pressure for 10 minutes.

Release the pressure naturally.

Discard the bay leaf and thyme stems.

Blend the soup using an immersion blender and serve!

Nutritional Values (Per Serving)

Calories: 454

Fat: 31 g

Carbohydrates: 7 g

Protein: 27 g

Elegant Zero Crust Kale and Mushroom Quiche

Preparation time: 5 minutes

Cooking time: 9 hours

Servings: 3

INGREDIENTS:

6 large eggs

2 tablespoons unsweetened almond milk

2 ounces low –fat feta cheese, crumbled

¼ cup parmesan cheese, grated

1½ teaspoons Italian seasoning

4 ounces mushrooms, sliced

2 cups kale, chopped

DIRECTIONS:

Grease the inner pot of your Ninja Foodi.

Take a large bowl and whisk in eggs, cheese, almond milk, seasoning and mix it well.

Stir in kale and mushrooms. Pour the mix into Ninja Foodi. Gently stir.

Place lid and cook on Slow Cook Mode (low) for 8-9 hours. Serve and enjoy!

Nutritional Values (Per Serving)

Calories: 112

Fat: 7 g

Carbohydrates: 4 g

Protein: 10 g

Delicious Beet Borscht

Preparation time: 5 minutes

Cooking time: 45 minutes

Servings: 3

INGREDIENTS:

8 cups beets

½ cup celery, diced

½ cup carrots, diced

2 garlic cloves, diced

1 medium onion, diced

3 cups cabbage, shredded

6 cups beef stock

1 bay leaf

1 tablespoon salt

½ tablespoon thyme

¼ cup fresh dill, chopped

½ cup of coconut yogurt

DIRECTIONS:

Add the washed beets to a steamer in the Ninja Foodi.

Add 1 cup of water. Steam for 7 minutes.

Perform a quick release and drop into an ice bath.

Carefully peel off the skin and dice the beets.

Transfer the diced beets, celery, carrots, onion, garlic, cabbage, stock, bay leaf, thyme, and salt to your Instant Pot. Lock up the lid and set the pot to Soup mode, cook for 45 minutes.

Release the pressure naturally. Transfer to bowls and top with a dollop of dairy-free yogurt.

Enjoy with a garnish of fresh dill!

Nutritional Values (Per Serving)

Calories: 625

Fats: 46 g

Carbs: 19 g

Protein: 90 g

Pepper Jack Cauliflower Meal

Preparation time: 5 minutes

Cooking time: 3 hours 35 minutes

Servings: 3

INGREDIENTS:

1 head cauliflower

¼ cup whipping cream

4 ounces cream cheese

½ teaspoon pepper

1 teaspoon salt

2 tablespoons butter

4 ounces pepper jack cheese

6 bacon slices, crumbled

DIRECTIONS:

Grease the Ninja Foodi and add listed ingredients (except cheese and bacon).

Stir and Lock the lid, cook Slow Cook Mode (low) for 3 hours.

Remove lid and add cheese, stir. Lock the lid again and cook for 1 hour more.

Garnish with bacon crumbles and enjoy!

Nutritional Values (Per Serving)

Calories: 272

Fat: 21 g

Carbohydrates: 5 g

Protein: 10 g

Slow-Cooked Brussels

Preparation time: 5 minutes

Cooking time: 4 hours

Servings: 3

INGREDIENTS:

1 lb. brussel sprouts, bottom trimmed and cut

1 tablespoon olive oil

1½ tablespoon Dijon mustard

¼ cup of water

Salt and pepper as needed

½ teaspoon dried tarragon

DIRECTIONS:

Add brussel sprouts, salt, water, pepper, mustard to the Ninja Foodi.

Add dried tarragon and stir.

Lock the lid and cook on Slow Cook Mode (low) for 5 hours until the sprouts are tender.

Stir well and add Dijon mustard over sprouts. Stir and enjoy!

Nutritional Values (Per Serving)

Calories: 83

Fat: 4 g

Carbohydrates: 11 g

Protein: 4 g

Honey Dressed Asparagus

Preparation Time: 5-10 minutes

Cooking Time: 15 minutes

Servings: 4

INGREDIENTS:

2 pounds asparagus, trimmed

4 tablespoons tarragon, minced

¼ cup honey

2 tablespoons olive oil

1 teaspoon salt

½ teaspoon pepper

DIRECTIONS:

Add asparagus, oil, salt, honey, pepper, tarragon into your bow. Toss them well.

Preheat your Ninja Foodi by pressing the Grill option and setting it to **MED**.

Set the timer to 8 minutes.

Allow it preheat until it makes a beep sound.

Arrange asparagus over grill grate and lock the lid.

Cook for 4 minutes.

Then flip asparagus and cook for 4 minutes more.

Serve and enjoy!

Nutritional Values (Per Serving)

Calories: 240

Fat: 15 g

Saturated Fat: 3 g

Carbohydrates: 31 g

Fiber: 1 g

Sodium: 103 mg

Protein: 7 g

Italian Squash Meal

Preparation Time: 5-10 minutes

Cooking Time: 16 minutes

Servings: 4

INGREDIENTS:

1 medium butternut squash, peeled, seeded, and cut into ½-inch slices

1½ teaspoons oregano, dried

1 teaspoon dried thyme

1 tablespoon olive oil

½ teaspoon salt

¼ teaspoon black pepper

DIRECTIONS:

Add slices alongside other ingredients into a mixing bowl.

Mix them well.

Preheat your Ninja Foodi by pressing the Grill option and setting it to **MED**.

Set the timer to 16 minutes.

Allow it to preheat until it beeps.

Arrange squash slices over the grill grate.

Cook for 8 minutes.

Flip and cook for 8 minutes more.

Serve and enjoy!

Nutritional Values (Per Serving)

Calories: 238

Fat: 12 g

Saturated Fat: 2 g

Carbohydrates: 36 g

Fiber: 3 g

Sodium: 128 mg

Protein: 15 g

Air Grilled Brussels

Preparation Time: 5-10 minutes

Cooking Time: 12 minutes

Servings: 4

INGREDIENTS:

6 slices bacon, chopped

1-pound brussels sprouts, halved

2 tablespoons olive oil, extra virgin

1 teaspoon salt

½ teaspoon black pepper, ground

DIRECTIONS:

Add Brussels, olive oil, salt, pepper, and bacon into a mixing bowl.

Preheat the Ninja Foodi by pressing the Air Crisp option and setting it to 390°F.

Set the timer to 12 minutes.

Allow it to preheat until it beeps.

Arrange Brussels over basket and lock the lid.

Cook for 6 minutes.

Shake it and cook for 6 minutes more.

Serve and enjoy!

Nutritional Values (Per Serving)

Calories: 279

Fat: 18 g

Saturated Fat: 4 g

Carbohydrates: 12 g

Fiber: 4 g

Sodium: 874 mg

Slowly Cooked Lemon Artichokes

Preparation time: 10 minutes

Cooking time: 5 hours

Servings: 4

INGREDIENTS:

5 large artichokes

1 teaspoon of sea salt

2 stalks celery, sliced

2 large carrots, cut into matchsticks

Juice from 1/2 a lemon

¼ teaspoon black pepper

1 teaspoon dried thyme

1 tablespoon dried rosemary

Lemon wedges for garnish

DIRECTIONS:

Remove the stalk from your artichokes and remove the tough outer shell.

Transfer the chokes to your Ninja Foodi and add 2 cups of boiling water.

Add celery, lemon juice, salt, carrots, black pepper, thyme, rosemary.

Cook on Slow Cook mode (high) for 4-5 hours.

Serve the artichokes with lemon wedges. Serve and enjoy!

Nutritional Values (Per Serving)

Calories: 205

Fat: 2 g

Carbohydrates: 12 g

Protein: 34 g

Well Dressed Brussels

Preparation time: 10 minutes

Cooking time: 4-5 hours

Servings: 4

INGREDIENTS:

2 pounds Brussels, halved

2 red onions, sliced

2 tablespoons apple cider vinegar

1 tablespoon extra-virgin olive oil

1 teaspoon ground cinnamon

½ cup pecans, chopped

DIRECTIONS:

Add Brussels and onions to the Ninja Foodi. Take a small bowl and add cinnamon, vinegar, olive oil.

Pour mixture over sprouts and toss.

Place lid and cook on Slow Cook mode (low) for 4-5 hours. Enjoy!

Nutritional Values (Per Serving)

Calories: 176

Fat: 10 g

Carbohydrates: 14 g

Protein: 4 g

Cheddar Cauliflower Bowl

Preparation time: 10 minutes

Cooking time: 5 minutes

Servings: 4

INGREDIENTS:

¼ cup butter

½ sweet onion, chopped

1 head cauliflower, chopped

4 cups herbed vegetable stock

½ teaspoon ground nutmeg

1 cup heavy whip cream

Salt and pepper as needed

1 cup cheddar cheese, shredded

DIRECTIONS:

Set your Ninja Foodi to sauté mode and add butter, let it heat up, and melt.

Add onion and cauliflower. Sauté for 10 minutes until tender and lightly browned.

Add vegetable stock and nutmeg, bring to a boil.

Lock the lid and cook on high pressure for 5 minutes, quick release pressure once done.

Remove the pot from the Foodi and stir in heavy cream. Puree using an immersion blender.

Season with more salt and pepper and serve with a topping of cheddar. Enjoy!

Nutritional Values (Per Serving)

Calories: 227

Fat: 21 g

Carbohydrates: 4 g

Protein: 8 g

A Prosciutto and Thyme Eggs

Preparation time: 10 minutes

Cooking time: 5 minutes

Servings: 5

INGREDIENTS:

4 kale leaves

4 prosciutto slices

3 tablespoons heavy cream

4 hardboiled eggs

¼ teaspoon pepper

¼ teaspoon salt

1½ cups of water

DIRECTIONS:

Peel eggs and wrap in kale. Wrap in prosciutto and sprinkle salt and pepper.

Add water to your Ninja Foodi and lower trivet. Place eggs inside and lock the lid.

Cook on HIGH pressure for 5 minutes. Quick-release pressure. Serve and enjoy!

Nutritional Values (Per Serving)

Calories: 290

Fat: 23 g

Carbohydrates: 4 g

Protein: 16 g

The Authentic Zucchini Pesto Meal

Preparation time: 10 minutes

Cooking time: 10 minutes

Servings: 8

INGREDIENTS:

1 tablespoon olive oil

1 onion, chopped

2½ pound roughly chopped zucchini

½ cup of water

1½ teaspoon salt

1 bunch basil leaves

2 garlic cloves, minced

1 tablespoon extra-virgin olive oil

Zucchini for making zoodles

DIRECTIONS:

Set the Ninja Foodi to Sauté mode and add olive oil.

Once the oil is hot, add onion and sauté for 4 minutes.

Add zucchini, water, and salt. Lock up the lid and cook on high pressure for 3 minutes.

Release the pressure naturally. Add basil, garlic, and leaves.

Use an immersion blender to blend everything well until you have a sauce-like consistency.

Take the extra zucchini and pass them through a Spiralizer to get noodle-like shapes.

Toss the zoodles with sauce and enjoy!

Nutritional Values (Per Serving)

Calories: 71

Fat: 4 g

Carbohydrates: 6 g

Protein: 3 g

Supreme Cauliflower Soup

Preparation time: 10 minutes

Cooking time: 5 minutes

Servings: 4

INGREDIENTS:

½ a small onion, chopped

2 tablespoons butter

1 large head of cauliflower, leaves and stems removed, coarsely chopped

2 cups chicken stock

1 teaspoon garlic powder

1 teaspoon salt

4 ounces cream cheese, cut into cubes

1 cup sharp cheddar cheese, cut

1/2 cup cream

Extra cheddar, sour cream bacon strips, green onion for topping

DIRECTIONS:

Peel the onion and chop up into small pieces.

Cut the leaves of the cauliflower and steam, making sure to keep the core intact.

Coarsely chop the cauliflower into pieces.

Set your Ninja Foodi to Sauté mode and add onion, cook for 2-3 minutes.

Add chopped cauliflower, stock, salt, and garlic powder.

Lock up the lid and cook on high pressure for 5 minutes. Perform a quick release.

Prepare the toppings. Use an immersion blender to puree your soup in the Ninja Foodi.

Serve your soup with a topping of sliced green onions, cheddar, crumbled bacon. Enjoy!

Nutritional Values (Per Serving)

Calories: 438

Fat: 36 g

Carbohydrates: 8 g

Protein: 22 g

Very Rich and Creamy Asparagus Soup

Preparation time: 10 minutes

Cooking time: 5-10 minutes

Servings: 3

INGREDIENTS:

1 tablespoon olive oil

3 green onions, sliced crosswise into ¼ inch pieces

1 lb. asparagus, tough ends removed, cut into 1-inch pieces

4 cups vegetable stock

1 tablespoon unsalted butter

1 tablespoon almond flour

2 teaspoon salt

1 teaspoon white pepper

½ cup heavy cream

DIRECTIONS:

Set your Ninja Foodi to Sauté mode and add oil, let it heat up.

Add green onions and Sauté for a few minutes, add asparagus and stock.

Lock the lid and cook on high pressure for 5 minutes.

Take a small saucepan and place it over low heat, add butter, flour and stir until the mixture foams and turns into a golden beige, this is your blond roux.

Remove from heat. Release pressure naturally over 10 minutes.

Open the lid and add roux, salt, and pepper to the soup.

Use an immersion blender to puree the soup.

Taste and season accordingly, swirl in cream, and enjoy!

Nutritional Values (Per Serving)

Calories: 192

Fat: 14 g

Carbohydrates: 8 g

Protein: 6 g

Delicious Cajun Eggplant

Preparation Time: 5-10 minutes

Cooking Time: 12 minutes

Servings: 4

INGREDIENTS:

¼ cup olive oil

2 small eggplants, cut into slices

3 teaspoons Cajun seasoning

2 tablespoons lime juice

DIRECTIONS:

Coat eggplant slices with oil, lemon juice, and Cajun seasoning.

Take your Ninja Foodi Grill and press **Grill** and set to Med mode, set the timer to 10 minutes.

Let it preheat.

Arrange eggplants over grill grate, lock the lid, and cook for 5 minutes.

Flip and cook for 5 minutes more.

Serve and enjoy!

Nutritional Values (Per Serving)

Calories: 362

Fat: 11 g

Saturated Fat: 3 g

Carbohydrates: 16 g

Fiber: 1 g

Sodium: 694 mg

Protein: 8 g

Roasted Mixed Veggies

Preparation Time: 15 minutes

Cooking Time: 15 minutes

Servings: 4

INGREDIENTS:

1 zucchini, sliced

8 oz. mushrooms, sliced

2 tablespoons olive oil

1 tablespoon garlic, minced

1 teaspoon onion powder

1 teaspoon garlic powder

Salt and pepper to taste

DIRECTIONS:

Choose the Air Fry setting on your Ninja Foodi Grill.

Insert air fryer basket.

Preheat it to 390°F.

Toss zucchini and mushrooms in oil.

Sprinkle with garlic.

Season with onion powder, garlic powder, salt, and pepper.

Place in the basket.

Cook for 10 minutes.

Stir and cook for another 5 minutes.

Serving Suggestions:

Serve as a side dish to the main course.

Preparation/Cooking Tips:

Do not overcrowd the basket with veggies.

Nutritional Values (Per Serving)

Calories: 345

Fat: 30 g

Carbohydrates: 5 g

Protein: 20 g

Mediterranean Veggies

Preparation Time: 30 minutes

Cooking Time: 20 minutes

Servings: 6

INGREDIENTS:

1 zucchini, sliced

2 tomatoes, sliced in half

1 red bell pepper, sliced

1 orange bell pepper, sliced

1 yellow bell pepper, sliced

3 oz. black olives

1 tablespoon olive oil

1 teaspoon dried parsley

1 teaspoon dried oregano

1 teaspoon dried basil leaves

Salt and pepper to taste

6 cloves garlic, minced

DIRECTIONS:

Combine all the ingredients in a large bowl.

Transfer to the air fryer basket.

Insert air fryer basket to your Ninja Foodi Grill.

Select the Air Fry setting.

Cook at 390°F for 10 minutes.

Stir and cook for another 10 minutes.

Serving Suggestions:

Serve with crumbled feta cheese.

Preparation/Cooking Tips:

Add other colorful veggies to this recipe.

Nutritional Values (Per Serving)

Calories: 390

Fat: 30 g

Carbohydrates: 10 g

Protein: 19 g

Chapter 4: Chicken and Poultry Recipes

Honey & Rosemary Chicken

Preparation Time: 15 minutes

Cooking Time: 35 minutes

Servings: 6

INGREDIENTS:

1 teaspoon paprika

Salt to taste

½ teaspoon baking powder

2 lb. chicken wings

¼ cup honey

1 tablespoon lemon juice

1 tablespoon garlic, minced

1 tablespoon rosemary, chopped

DIRECTIONS:

Choose the Air Fry setting on your Ninja Foodi Grill.

Set it to 390°F.

Set the time to 30 minutes.

Press **Start** to preheat.

While waiting, mix the paprika, salt, and baking powder in a bowl.

Add the wings to the crisper basket.

Close and cook for 15 minutes.

Flip and cook for another 15 minutes.

In a bowl, mix the remaining ingredients.

Coat the wings with the sauce and cook for another 5 minutes.

Serving Suggestions: Serve with the remaining sauce.

Preparation/Cooking Tips:

You can also add crushed red pepper to the spice mixture.

Nutritional Values (Per Serving)

Calories: 438

Fat: 36 g

Carbohydrates: 8 g

Protein: 22 g

Grilled Chicken with Veggies

Preparation Time: 20 minutes

Cooking Time: 25 minutes

Servings: 2

INGREDIENTS:

2 chicken thighs and legs

2 tablespoons oil, divided

Salt and pepper to taste

1 onion, diced

¼ cup mushrooms, sliced

1 cup potatoes, diced

1 tablespoon lemon juice

1 tablespoon honey

4 sprigs fresh thyme, chopped

2 cloves garlic, crushed and minced

DIRECTIONS:

Add the grill grate to your Ninja Foodi Grill.

Put the veggie tray on top of the grill grate.

Close the hood.

Choose the grill function and set it to high.

Press **Start** to preheat.

Brush the chicken with half of the oil.

Season with salt and pepper.

Toss the onion, mushrooms, and potatoes in the remaining oil.

Sprinkle with salt and pepper.

Add chicken to the grill grate.

Add the potato mixture to the veggie tray.

Close the hood and cook for 10 to 15 minutes.

Flip chicken and toss potatoes.

Cook for another 10 minutes.

Serving Suggestions:

Serve chicken with the veggies on the side. Garnish with herb sprigs.

Preparation/Cooking Tips:

Add more cooking time if you want skin crispier.

Nutritional Values (Per Serving)

Calories: 178

Fat: 13 g

Carbohydrates: 6 g

Protein: 20 g

Excellent Chicken Tomatino

Preparation Time: 5-10 minutes

Cooking Time: 12 minutes

Servings: 4

INGREDIENTS:

½ teaspoon salt

1 garlic clove, minced

2 tablespoons olive oil

¾ cup vinegar

8 plum tomatoes

¼ cup fresh basil leaves

4 chicken breast, boneless and skinless

DIRECTIONS:

Take your fine food processor and add olive oil, vinegar, salt, garlic, and basil. Blend the mixture well until you have a smooth texture.

Add tomatoes and blend once again.

Take a mixing bowl and add tomato mix, chicken and mix well.

Let the mixture chill for 1-2 hours.

Preheat your Ninja Foodi Grill to High and set the timer to 6 minutes.

Once you hear the beep, arrange your prepared chicken over the grill grate.

Cook for 3 minutes more.

Flip the chicken and cook for 3 minutes more.

Once properly cooked, serve and enjoy!

Nutritional Values (Per Serving)

Calories: 400

Fat: 5 g

Saturated Fat: 3 g

Carbohydrates: 18 g

Fiber: 3 g

Sodium: 230 mg

Protein: 23 g

Majestic Alfredo Chicken

Preparation Time: 5-10 minutes

Cooking Time: 20 minutes

Servings: 4

INGREDIENTS:

½ cup alfredo sauce

¼ cup blue cheese, crumbled

4 slices provolone cheese

4 teaspoons chicken seasoning

4 chicken breasts, halved

1 tablespoon lemon juice

1 large apple wedged

DIRECTIONS:

Take a medium-sized bowl and add chicken, alongside the seasoning.

Take another bowl and toss the apple with lemon.

Preheat your Ninja Foodi Grill in **Med** mode, set timer to 16 minutes.

Wait until you hear a beep sound.

Arrange chicken pieces to the grill grate and cook for about 8 minutes, flip and cook for 8 minutes.

Transfer the apple to the grill and cook for 4 minutes, giving 2 minutes to each side.

Serve grilled chicken with the blue cheese, apple, and alfredo sauce.

Enjoy!

Nutritional Values (Per Serving)

Calories: 247

Fat: 19 g

Saturated Fat: 3 g

Carbohydrates: 29 g

Fiber: 2 g

Sodium: 850 mg

Protein: 14 g

Chicken Parmesan

Preparation Time: 5-10 minutes

Cooking Time: 20 minutes

Servings: 4

INGREDIENTS:

2 chicken breasts, sliced into cutlets

6 tablespoons seasoned bread crumbs

2 tablespoons Parmesan cheese, grated

1 tablespoon butter, melted

6 tablespoons reduced-fat mozzarella cheese

½ cup marinara sauce

Cooking spray

DIRECTIONS:

Spray the Ninja Foodi basket with oil.

In a bowl, mix the bread crumbs and Parmesan cheese. In another bowl, place the butter. Coat the chicken with butter and dip into the bread crumb mix.

Place the cutlets on the basket. Seal the crisping lid. Set it to **Air Cris**p.

Cook at 375°F for 6 minutes.

Flip and top with the marinara and mozzarella.

Serving Suggestion:

Serve with pasta or salad.

Tips:

Use whole-wheat bread crumbs.

Nutritional Information Per Serving:

Calories: 307

Total Fat: 14.4 g

Saturated Fat: 6.5 g

Cholesterol: 87 mg

Sodium: 599 mg

Total Carbohydrate: 13.3 g

Dietary Fiber: 1.4 g

Total Sugars: 3.4 g

Protein: 30.8 g

Potassium: 303 mg

Honey Chicken Wings

Preparation Time: 5-10 minutes

Cooking Time: 20 minutes

Servings: 4

INGREDIENTS:

1 lb. chicken wings

¼ cup honey

2 tablespoons hot sauce

1½ tablespoons soy sauce

1 tablespoon butter

1 tablespoon lime juice

DIRECTIONS:

Place the chicken wings in the Ninja Foodi basket. Add the basket to the pot.

Cover the crisping lid. Set it to **Air Crisp**. Cook at 360°F for 30 minutes.

Flip every 10 minutes. Remove the wings and set aside. Set the pot to **Sauté**.

Add the rest of the ingredients and mix well. Simmer for 3 minutes.

Toss the wings in the mixture before serving.

Serving Suggestion:

Garnish with chopped chives.

Tips:

Use freshly squeezed lime juice.

Nutritional Information Per Serving:

Calories: 619

Total Fat: 22.6 g

Saturated Fat: 8.3 g

Cholesterol: 217 mg

Sodium: 1295 mg

Total Carbohydrate: 36.1 g

Dietary Fiber: 0.2 g

Total Sugars: 35.2 g

Protein: 66.6 g

Potassium: 622 mg

Chicken Nuggets

Preparation Time: 5-10 minutes

Cooking Time: 40 minutes

Servings: 4

INGREDIENTS:

2 teaspoons olive oil

6 tablespoons breadcrumbs

2 tablespoons grated parmesan cheese

2 chicken breasts, sliced into nuggets

Salt and pepper to taste

Cooking spray

DIRECTIONS:

Pour the olive oil into one bowl.

In another bowl, mix the bread crumbs and Parmesan.

Season the chicken with salt and pepper.

Coat with the olive oil and dip in the bread crumb mixture.

Place the chicken on the basket. Seal the crisping lid. Select **Air Crisp**.

Cook at 375°F for 8 minutes.

Serving Suggestion:

Serve with a green salad or veggie sticks.

Tips:

Use whole-wheat bread crumbs.

Nutritional Information Per Serving:

Calories: 245

Total Fat: 11.4 g

Saturated Fat: 4 g

Cholesterol: 75 mg

Sodium: 267 mg

Total Carbohydrate: 7.8 g

Dietary Fiber: 0.5 g

Total Sugars: 0.6 g

Protein: 27 g

Potassium: 198 mg

Peanut Chicken

Preparation Time: 5-10 minutes

Cooking Time: 20 minutes

Servings: 4

INGREDIENTS:

1½ lb. chicken breast, sliced into cubes

Salt to taste

1 teaspoon oil

3 clove garlic, chopped

1 tablespoon ginger, chopped

13 oz. coconut milk

3 tablespoons soy sauce

3 tablespoons honey

2 tablespoons fresh lime juice

1 tablespoon chili garlic paste

½ cup peanut butter

DIRECTIONS:

Season the chicken with salt. Set the Ninja Foodi to **Sauté**. Add the oil.

Cook the garlic and ginger for 1 minute.

Add the chicken and all the other ingredients except the peanut butter.

Mix well. Put the peanut butter on top of the chicken but do not stir.

Seal the pot. Set it to **Pressure**. Cook at high pressure for 9 minutes.

Release the pressure naturally.

Serving Suggestion:

Serve on top of spinach leaves.

Tips:

Spread peanut butter evenly on top of the chicken.

Nutritional Information Per Serving:

Calories: 445

Total Fat: 29.1 g

Saturated Fat: 15.4 g

Cholesterol: 73 mg

Sodium: 645 mg

Total Carbohydrate: 18 g

Dietary Fiber: 2.9 g

Total Sugars: 12.9 g

Protein: 31.5 g

Potassium: 762 mg

Honey Teriyaki Chicken

Preparation Time: 5-10 minutes

Cooking Time: 20 minutes

Servings: 4

INGREDIENTS:

4 chicken breasts, sliced into strips

1 cup soy sauce

½ cup water

2/3 cup honey

2 teaspoons garlic, minced

½ cup rice vinegar

½ teaspoon ground ginger

¼ teaspoon crushed red pepper flakes

3 tablespoons corn starch dissolved in 3 tablespoons cold water

DIRECTIONS:

Put the chicken inside the Ninja Foodi.

Add the rest of the ingredients except the corn starch mixture.

Put on the lid. Set it to **Pressure**. Cook at high pressure for 30 minutes.

Release the pressure naturally. Set it to **Sauté**.

Stir in the corn starch and simmer until the sauce has thickened.

Serving Suggestion:

Garnish with sesame seeds and serve with fried rice.

Tips:

Use low sodium soy sauce.

Nutritional Information Per Serving:

Calories: 495

Total Fat: 10.4 g

Saturated Fat: 2.9 g

Cholesterol: 125 mg

Sodium: 717 mg

Total Carbohydrate: 52.1 g

Dietary Fiber: 0.7 g

Total Sugars: 47.5 g

Protein: 44.8 g

Potassium: 519 mg

Feisty Hot Pepper Wings Delight

Preparation Time: 5-10 minutes

Cooking Time: 25 minutes

Servings: 4

INGREDIENTS:

½ cup hot pepper sauce

2 tablespoons butter, melted

1 tablespoon coconut oil

1-pound chicken wings

1 tablespoon ranch salad dressing

½ teaspoon paprika

DIRECTIONS:

Take a bowl and add chicken, oil, ranch dressing, and paprika. Transfer to your fridge and let it chill for about 30-60 minutes.

Take another bowl and add the pepper sauce alongside butter.

Preheat your Ninja Foodi Grill in **Med** mode, with a timer set to 25 minutes.

Arrange the chicken wings over the grill grate.

Cook for 25 minutes.

Serve once done with the pepper sauce.

Enjoy!

Nutritional Values (Per Serving)

Calories: 510

Fat: 24 g

Saturated Fat: 7 g

Carbohydrates: 6 g

Fiber: 0.5 g

Sodium: 841 mg

Protein: 54 g

Grilled Garlic Chicken

Preparation Time: 10 minutes

Cooking Time: 20 minutes

Servings: 8

INGREDIENTS:

3 lb. chicken thigh fillets

Garlic salt to taste

DIRECTIONS:

Add the grill plate to the Ninja Foodi Grill.

Preheat to medium heat.

Sprinkle chicken with garlic salt on both sides.

Cook for 8 to 10 minutes.

Flip and cook for another 7 minutes.

Serving Suggestions:

Serve with hot sauce and mustard and with fries on the side.

Preparation/Cooking Tips:

Add more cooking time to make the skin crispier.

Nutritional Values (Per Serving)

Calories: 278

Fat: 10 g

Carbohydrates: 6 g

Protein: 16 g

Grilled Balsamic Chicken Breast

Preparation Time: 45 minutes

Cooking Time: 45 minutes

Servings: 4

INGREDIENTS:

¼ cup olive oil

2 tablespoons balsamic vinegar

3 teaspoon garlic, minced

3 tablespoons soy sauce

1 tablespoon Worcestershire sauce

¼ cup brown sugar

Salt and pepper to taste

4 chicken breast fillets

DIRECTIONS:

In a bowl, mix all ingredients except chicken.

Reserve ¼ cup of the mixture for later.

Marinate the chicken breast in the remaining mixture for 30 minutes.

Add the grill grate to the Ninja Foodi Grill.

Set it to **Grill** and for 25 minutes.

Add the chicken breast and close the hood.

Cook for 10 minutes.

Flip and cook for another 5 minutes.

Baste with remaining sauce. Cook for 5 more minutes.

Serve with remaining sauce, if any.

Serving Suggestions:

Let chicken rest for 5 minutes before serving.

Preparation/Cooking Tips:

For thick chicken breast fillets, flatten with a meat mallet.

Nutritional Values (Per Serving)

Calories: 324

Fat: 25 g

Carbohydrates: 5 g

Protein: 17 g

A Genuine Hassel Back Chicken

Preparation time: 5 minutes

Cooking time: 60 minutes

Servings: 4

INGREDIENTS:

4 tablespoons butter

Salt and pepper to taste

2 cups fresh mozzarella cheese, thinly sliced

8 large chicken breasts

4 large Roma tomatoes, thinly sliced

DIRECTIONS:

Make a few deep slits in chicken breasts, and season with salt and pepper.

Stuff mozzarella cheese slices and tomatoes in chicken slits.

Grease Ninja Foodi pot with butter and arrange stuffed chicken breasts.

Lock the lid and **Bake/Roast** for 1 hour at 365°F. Serve and enjoy!

Nutritional Values (Per Serving)

Calories: 278

Fat: 15 g

Carbohydrates: 3.8 g

Protein: 15 g

Shredded Up Salsa Chicken

Preparation time: 5 minutes

Cooking time: 20 minutes

Servings: 4

INGREDIENTS:

1-pound chicken breast, skin and bones removed

¾ teaspoon cumin

½ teaspoon salt

Pinch of oregano

Pepper to taste

1 cup chunky salsa Keto friendly

DIRECTIONS:

Season chicken with spices and add to the Ninja Foodi.

Cover with salsa and lock the lid, cook on high pressure for 20 minutes.

Quick-release the pressure. Add chicken to a platter and shred the chicken. Serve and enjoy!

Nutritional Values (Per Serving)

Calories: 125

Fat: 3 g

Carbohydrates: 2 g

Protein: 22 g

1 teaspoon cumin

1 teaspoon garlic powder

Salt and pepper to taste

DIRECTIONS:

Add all ingredients to Ninja Foodi. Stir and lock the lid. Cook on high pressure for 10 minutes.

Release pressure naturally over 10 minutes. Serve and enjoy!

Nutritional Values (Per Serving)

Calories: 204

Fat: 14 g

Carbohydrates: 4 g

Protein: 14 g

Mexico's Favorite Chicken Soup

Preparation time: 5 minutes

Cooking time: 20 minutes

Servings: 4

INGREDIENTS:

2 cups chicken, shredded

4 tablespoons olive oil

½ cup cilantro, chopped

8 cups chicken broth

1/3 cup salsa

1 teaspoon onion powder

½ cup scallions, chopped

4 ounces green chilies, chopped

½ teaspoon habanero, minced

1 cup celery root, chopped

Taiwanese Chicken Delight

Preparation time: 5 minutes

Cooking time: 10 minutes

Servings: 4

INGREDIENTS:

6 dried red chilis

¼ cup sesame oil

2 tablespoons ginger

¼ cup garlic, minced

¼ cup red wine vinegar

¼ cup coconut aminos

Salt as needed

1.2 teaspoon Xanthan gum (for the finish)

¼ cup Thai basil, chopped

DIRECTIONS:

Set your Ninja Foodi to Sauté mode and add ginger, chilis, garlic. Sauté for 2 minutes.

Add remaining ingredients. Lock the lid and cook on high pressure for 10 minutes.

Quick-release the pressure. Serve and enjoy!

Nutritional Values (Per Serving)

Calories: 307

Fat: 15 g

Carbohydrates: 7 g

Protein: 31 g

Cabbage and Chicken Meatballs

Preparation time: 10 minutes + 30 minutes

Cooking time: 4-6 minutes

Servings: 4

INGREDIENTS:

1-pound ground chicken

¼ cup heavy whip cream

2 teaspoons salt

½ teaspoon ground caraway seeds

1½ teaspoons freshly ground black pepper, divided

¼ teaspoon ground allspice

4-6 cups green cabbage, thickly chopped

½ cup almond milk

2 tablespoons unsalted butter

DIRECTIONS:

Transfer meat to a bowl and add cream, 1 teaspoon salt, caraway, ½ teaspoon pepper, allspice, and mix it well. Let the mixture chill for 30 minutes

Once the mixture is ready, use your hands to scoop the mixture into meatballs.

Add half of your balls to the Ninja Foodi pot, and cover with half of the cabbage.

Add remaining balls and cover with the rest of the cabbage.

Add milk, pats of butter, season with salt and pepper.

Lock the lid and cook on high pressure for 4 minutes. Quick-release the pressure.

Unlock the lid and serve. Enjoy!

Nutritional Values (Per Serving)

Calories: 294

Fat: 26 g

Carbohydrates: 4 g

Protein: 12 g

Chapter 5: Fish and Seafood Recipes

Crumbed Flounder Fillet

Preparation Time: 10 minutes

Cooking Time: 12 minutes

Servings: 4

INGREDIENTS:

¼ cup vegetable oil

1 cup breadcrumbs

4 flounder fillets

1 egg, beaten

DIRECTIONS:

Set Ninja Foodi Grill to **Air Fry**.

Preheat to 350°F.

Combine oil and breadcrumbs in a bowl.

Mix until crumbly.

Coat the fish with the egg and dredge with the breadcrumb mixture.

Add fish fillets to the air fryer basket.

Cook for 12 minutes.

Serving Suggestions:

Garnish with lemon wedges.

Preparation/Cooking Tips:

You can also use olive oil in place of vegetable oil.

Nutritional Values (Per Serving)

Calories: 257

Fat: 19 g

Carbohydrates: 5 g

Protein: 14 g

Salmon with Coconut Aminos

Preparation Time: 45 minutes

Cooking Time: 15 minutes

Servings: 4

INGREDIENTS:

½ teaspoon ginger powder

½ teaspoon garlic powder

1 tablespoon honey

4 tablespoons coconut aminos

Salt and pepper to taste

3 salmon fillets

DIRECTIONS:

In a bowl, mix ginger powder, garlic powder, honey, coconut aminos, salt, and pepper in a bowl.

Coat the salmon fillets with this mixture.

Marinate for 30 minutes, covered in the refrigerator.

Add fish to the air fryer basket.

Set your Ninja Foodi Grill to **Air Fry**.

Cook at 390°F for 10 to 15 minutes.

Serving Suggestions:

Garnish with lemon slices.

Preparation/Cooking Tips:

Do not overcrowd the air fryer basket to ensure even cooking. Cook in batches if necessary.

Nutritional Values (Per Serving)

Calories: 400

Fat: 23 g

Carbohydrates: 6 g

Protein: 24 g

Lemon Garlic Shrimp

Preparation Time: 45 minutes

Cooking Time: 15 minutes

Servings: 4

INGREDIENTS:

1 lb. shrimp, peeled and deveined

1 tablespoon olive oil

4 cloves garlic, minced

1 tablespoon lemon juice

Salt to taste

DIRECTIONS:

Mix the olive oil, salt, lemon juice, and garlic. Toss shrimp in the mixture.

Marinate for 15 minutes. Place the shrimp in the Ninja Foodi basket.

Seal the crisping lid. Select the Air Crisp setting.

Cook at 350 degrees for 8 minutes. Flip and cook for 2 more minutes.

Serving Suggestion:

Sprinkle chopped parsley on top.

Tips:

Add crushed red pepper flakes if you like it spicy.

Nutritional Information Per Serving:

Calories: 170

Total Fat: 5.5 g

Saturated Fat: 1.1 g

Cholesterol: 239 mg

Sodium: 317 mg

Total Carbohydrate: 2.8 g

Dietary Fiber: 0.1 g

Total Sugars: 0.1 g

Protein: 26.1 g

Potassium: 209 mg

Crispy Cod Fish

Preparation Time: 45 minutes

Cooking Time: 15 minutes

Servings: 4

INGREDIENTS:

4 cod fish fillets

Salt and sugar to taste

1 teaspoon sesame oil

250 ml water

5 tablespoons light soy sauce

1 teaspoon dark soy sauce

3 tablespoons oil

5 slices ginger

DIRECTIONS:

Pat the cod fillets dry.

Season with the salt, sugar, and sesame oil. Marinate for 15 minutes.

Set the Ninja Foodi to **Air Crisp**.

Put the fish on top of the basket. Cook at 350°F for 3 minutes.

Flip and cook for 2 minutes. Take the fish out and set aside.

Put the rest of the ingredients in the pot.

Set it to **Sauté**. Simmer and pour over the fish before serving.

Serving Suggestion:

Top with chopped green onion.

Nutritional Information Per Serving:

Calories: 303

Total Fat: 13.1 g

Saturated Fat: 1.9 g

Cholesterol: 99 mg

Sodium: 144 mg

Total Carbohydrate: 2.9 g

Dietary Fiber: 0.5 g

Total Sugars: 0.1 g

Protein: 41.5 g

Potassium: 494 mg

Crispy Fish Nuggets

Preparation Time: 45 minutes

Cooking Time: 15 minutes

Servings: 4

INGREDIENTS:

1 lb. cod fillet, sliced into 8 pieces

Salt and pepper to taste

½ cup flour

1 tablespoon egg with 1 teaspoon water

1 cup bread crumbs

1 tablespoon vegetable oil

DIRECTIONS:

Season the fish with salt and pepper. Cover with the flour.

Dip the fish in the egg wash and into the bread crumbs.

Place the fish nuggets in the Ninja Foodi basket. Set it to **Air Crisp**.

Seal with the crisping lid. Cook at 360°F for 15 minutes.

Serving Suggestion:

Serve with lemon honey tartar sauce.

Tips:

Add dried dill or garlic powder to the seasoning to make it tastier.

Nutritional Information Per Serving:

Calories: 234

Total Fat: 5.4 g

Saturated Fat: 1 g

Cholesterol: 25 mg

Sodium: 229 mg

Total Carbohydrate: 31.4 g

Dietary Fiber: 1.7 g

Total Sugars: 1.7 g

Protein: 14.1 g

Potassium: 70 mg

Heartfelt Sesame Fish

Preparation time: 8 minutes

Cooking time: 8 minutes

Servings: 8

INGREDIENTS:

1½ pound salmon fillet

1 teaspoon sesame seeds

1 teaspoon butter, melted

½ teaspoon salt

1 tablespoon apple cider vinegar

¼ teaspoon rosemary, dried

DIRECTIONS:

Take apple cider vinegar and spray it onto the salmon fillets.

Then add dried rosemary, sesame seeds, butter, and salt.

Mix them well. Take butter sauce and brush the salmon properly.

Place the salmon on the rack and lower the air fryer lid. Set to Air Fry mode.

Cook the fish for 8 minutes at 360°F. Serve hot and enjoy!

Nutritional Values (Per Serving)

Calories: 239

Fat: 11.2 g

Carbohydrates: 0.3 g

Protein: 33.1 g

Awesome Sockeye Salmon

Preparation time: 5 minutes

Cooking time: 5 minutes

Servings: 8

INGREDIENTS:

4 sockeye salmon fillets

1 teaspoon Dijon mustard

¼ teaspoon garlic, minced

¼ teaspoon onion powder

¼ teaspoon lemon pepper

½ teaspoon garlic powder

¼ teaspoon salt

2 tablespoons olive oil

1½ cup of water

DIRECTIONS:

Take a bowl and add mustard, lemon juice, onion powder, lemon pepper, garlic powder, salt, olive oil. Brush spice mix over salmon.

Add water to Instant Pot. Place the rack inside and place salmon fillets on rack.

Lock the lid and cook on low pressure for 7 minutes.

Quickly release the pressure. Serve and enjoy!

Nutritional Values (Per Serving)

Calories: 353

Fat: 25 g

Carbohydrates: 0.6 g

Protein: 40 g

Easy Fish Stew

Preparation Time: 5 minutes

Cooking Time: 20 minutes

Servings: 4

INGREDIENTS:

1 pound white fish fillets, chopped

1 cup broccoli, chopped

3 cups fish stock

1 onion, diced

2 cups celery stalks, chopped

1 cup heavy cream

1 bay leaf

1½ cups cauliflower, diced

1 carrot, sliced

2 tablespoons butter

¼ teaspoon garlic powder

½ teaspoon salt

¼ teaspoon pepper

DIRECTIONS:

Set your Ninja Foodi to Sauté.

Add butter, and let it melt.

Add onion and carrots, cook for 3 minutes.

Stir in remaining ingredients.

Close the lid.

Cook for 4 minutes on **High**.

Release the pressure naturally over 10 minutes.

Remove the bay leave once cooked.

Serve and enjoy!

Nutritional Values (Per Serving)

Calories: 298 g

Fat: 18 g

Saturated Fat: 3 g

Carbohydrates: 6 g

Fiber: 2 g

Sodium: 846 mg

Protein: 24 g

Buttery Scallops

Preparation Time: 10 minutes

Cooking Time: 5 minutes

Servings: 4

INGREDIENTS:

2 pounds sea scallops

½ cup butter

4 garlic cloves, minced

4 tablespoons rosemary, chopped

Salt and pepper to taste

DIRECTIONS:

Set your Ninja Foodi to **Sauté**.

Add rosemary, garlic, and butter. Sauté for 1 minute.

Add scallops, salt, and pepper. Sauté for 2 minutes.

Close the crisping lid.

Cook for 3 minutes to 350°F.

Serve and enjoy!

Nutritional Values (Per Serving)

Calories: 278 g

Fat: 15 g

Saturated Fat: 4 g

Carbohydrates: 5 g

Fiber: 2 g

Sodium: 502 mg

Protein: 25 g

lovely Air Fried Scallops

Preparation Time: 5 minutes

Cooking Time: 5 minutes

Servings: 4

INGREDIENTS:

12 scallops

3 tablespoons olive oil

Salt and pepper, to taste

DIRECTIONS:

Rub the scallops with salt, pepper, and olive oil.

Transfer it to the Ninja Foodi.

Place the insert in your Ninja Foodi.

Close the air crisping lid.

Cook for 4 minutes at 390°F.

Flip them after 2 minutes.

Serve and enjoy!

Nutritional Values (Per Serving)

Calories: 372 g

Fat: 11 g

Saturated Fat: 3 g

Carbohydrates: 0.9 g

Fiber: 0 g

Sodium: 750 mg

Protein: 63 g

Sweet and Sour Fish

Preparation Time: 10 minutes

Cooking Time: 6 minutes

Servings: 4

INGREDIENTS:

1 pound fish chunks

1 tablespoon vinegar

2 drops liquid Stevia

¼ cup butter

Salt and pepper to taste

DIRECTIONS:

Set your Ninja Foodi to **Sauté**.

Add butter and melt it.

Add fish chunks, sauté for 3 minutes.

Add Stevia, salt, pepper, stir it.

Close the crisping lid.

Cook on Air Crisp mode for 3 minutes at 360°F

Serve and enjoy!

Nutritional Values (Per Serving)

Calories: 274 g

Fat: 15 g

Saturated Fat: 4 g

Carbohydrates: 2 g

Fiber: 0 g

Sodium: 896 mg

Protein: 33 g

Buttered Up Scallops

Preparation time: 10 minutes

Cooking time: 5 minutes

Servings: 8

INGREDIENTS:

4 garlic cloves, minced

4 tablespoons rosemary, chopped

2 pounds sea scallops

½ cup butter

Salt and pepper to taste

DIRECTIONS:

Set your Ninja Foodi to **Sauté** and add butter, rosemary, and garlic.

Sauté for 1 minute. Add scallops, salt, and pepper.

Sauté for 2 minutes. Lock the crisping lid and crisp for 3 minutes at 350°F. Serve and enjoy!

Nutritional Values (Per Serving)

Calories: 279

Fat: 16 g

Carbohydrates: 5 g

Protein: 25 g

Awesome Cherry Tomato Mackerel

Preparation time: 5 minutes

Cooking time: 7 minutes

Servings: 8

INGREDIENTS:

4 Mackerel fillets

¼ teaspoon onion powder

¼ teaspoon lemon powder

¼ teaspoon garlic powder

½ teaspoon salt

2 cups cherry tomatoes

3 tablespoons melted butter

1½ cups of water

1 tablespoon black olives

DIRECTIONS:

Grease baking dish and arrange cherry tomatoes at the bottom of the dish.

Top with fillets. Sprinkle all spices. Drizzle melted butter on top.

Add water to the lower rack in the Ninja Foodi and place a baking dish on top of the rack.

Lock the lid and cook on low pressure for 7 minutes. Quickly release the pressure. Serve and enjoy!

Nutritional Values (Per Serving)

Calories: 325

Fat: 24 g

Carbohydrates: 2 g

Protein: 21 g

Lovely Air Fried Scallops

Preparation time: 5 minutes

Cooking time: 5 minutes

Servings: 8

INGREDIENTS:

12 scallops

3 tablespoons olive oil

Salt and pepper to taste

DIRECTIONS:

Gently rub scallops with salt, pepper, and oil

Transfer to the insert in the Ninja Foodi.

Lock the air crisping lid and cook for 4 minutes at 390°F.

Half through, make sure to give them a nice flip and keep cooking. Serve warm and enjoy!

Nutritional Values (Per Serving)

Calories: 372

Fat: 11 g

Carbohydrates: 0.9 g

Protein: 63 g

Packets of Lemon and Dill Cod

Preparation time: 10 minutes

Cooking time: 5-10 minutes

Servings: 8

INGREDIENTS:

2 tilapia cod fillets

Salt, pepper, and garlic powder to taste

2 sprigs fresh dill

4 slices lemon

2 tablespoons butter

DIRECTIONS:

Lay out two large squares of parchment paper.

Place fillet in center of each parchment square and season with salt, pepper, and garlic powder.

On each fillet, place 1 sprig of dill, 2 lemon slices, and 1 tablespoon butter.

Place trivet at the bottom of your Ninja Foodi. Add 1 cup water into the pot.

Close parchment paper around fillets and fold to make a nice seal.

Place both packets in your pot. Lock the lid and cook on high pressure for 5 minutes.

Quickly release the pressure. Serve and enjoy!

Nutritional Values (Per Serving)

Calories: 259

Fat: 11 g

Carbohydrates: 8 g

Protein: 20 g

Adventurous Sweet and Sour Fish

Preparation time: 10 minutes

Cooking time: 6 minutes

Servings: 8

INGREDIENTS:

2 drops liquid Stevia

¼ cup butter

1 pound fish chunks

1 tablespoon vinegar

Salt and pepper to taste

DIRECTIONS:

Set your Ninja Foodi to Sauté mode. Add butter and let it melt.

Add fish chunks and Sauté for 3 minutes. Add Stevia, salt, and pepper and stir.

Lock the crisping lid and cook on Air Crisp mode for 3 minutes at 360°F.

Serve once done and enjoy!

Nutritional Values (Per Serving)

Calories: 274

Fat: 15 g

Carbohydrates: 2 g

Protein: 33 g

Garlic and Lemon Prawn Delight

Preparation time: 5 minutes

Cooking time: 5 minutes

Servings: 8

INGREDIENTS:

2 tablespoons olive oil

1 pound prawns

2 tablespoons garlic, minced

2/3 cup fish stock

1 tablespoon butter

2 tablespoons lemon juice

1 tablespoon lemon zest

Salt and pepper to taste

DIRECTIONS:

Set your Ninja Foodi to Sauté mode and add butter and oil. Let it heat up.

Stir in remaining ingredients. Lock the lid and cook on low pressure for 5 minutes.

Quick-release the pressure. Serve and enjoy!

Nutritional Values (Per Serving)

Calories: 236

Fat: 12 g

Carbohydrates: 2 g

Protein: 27 g

Lovely Carb Soup

Preparation time: 5 minutes

Cooking time: 6-7 hours

Servings: 4

INGREDIENTS:

1 cup crab meat, cubed

1 tablespoon garlic, minced

Salt as needed

Red chili flakes as needed

3 cups vegetable broth

1 teaspoon salt

DIRECTIONS:

Coat the crab cubes in lime juice and let them sit for a while.

Add the all ingredients (including marinated crab meat) to your Ninja Foodi and lock the lid.

Cook on Slow Cook mode (medium) for 3 hours.

Let it sit for a while.

Unlock the lid and set to Sauté mode, simmer the soup for 5 minutes more on Low.

Stir and check seasoning. Enjoy!

Nutritional Values (Per Serving)

Calories: 201

Fat: 11 g

Carbohydrates: 12 g

Protein: 13 g

The Rich Guy Lobster and Butter

Preparation time: 15 minutes

Cooking time: 20 minutes

Servings: 8

INGREDIENTS:

6 lobster tails

4 garlic cloves,

¼ cup butter

DIRECTIONS:

Preheat the Ninja Foodi to 400°F at first.

Open the lobster tails gently by using kitchen scissors.

Remove the lobster meat gently from the shells but keep it inside the shells.

Take a plate and place it.

Add some butter to a pan and allow it melt.

Put some garlic cloves in it and heat it over medium-low heat.

Pour the garlic butter mixture all over the lobster tail meat.

Let the fryer to broil the lobster at 130°F.

Remove the lobster meat from Ninja Foodi and set aside.

Use a fork to pull out the lobster meat from the shells entirely.

Pour some garlic butter over it if needed. Serve and enjoy!

Nutritional Values (Per Serving)

Calories: 160

Fat: 1 g

Carbohydrates: 1 g

Protein: 20 g

Beer-Battered Cod

Preparation Time: 15 minutes

Cooking Time: 15 minutes

Servings: 4

INGREDIENTS:

1 cup all-purpose flour

½ teaspoon baking soda

2 tablespoons cornstarch

1 egg, beaten

6 oz. beer

4 cod fillets

½ teaspoon paprika

Pinch cayenne pepper

Salt and pepper to taste

Vegetable oil

DIRECTIONS:

Mix flour, baking soda, cornstarch, egg, and beer in a bowl.

Sprinkle cod fillets with paprika, cayenne, salt, and pepper.

Dip in the flour mixture.

Drizzle with oil.

Add to the air fryer basket.

Choose the Air Fry setting on your Ninja Foodi Grill.

Cook at 390°F for 12-15 minutes.

Serving Suggestions:

Serve with coleslaw.

Preparation/Cooking Tips:

Refrigerate flour mixture for 20 minutes before using it.

Nutritional Values (Per Serving)

Calories: 438

Fat: 36 g

Carbohydrates: 8 g

Protein: 22 g

Grilled Shrimp

Preparation Time: 20 minutes

Cooking Time: 10 minutes

Servings: 8

INGREDIENTS:

2 lb. shrimp, de-veined

2 tablespoons olive oil

1 tablespoon Old Bay seasoning

Garlic salt to taste

DIRECTIONS:

Preheat your grill to medium.

Brush shrimp with olive oil.

Season with Old Bay seasoning and garlic salt.

Cook for 3-5 minutes per side.

Serving Suggestions:

Serve with grilled corn.

Preparation/Cooking Tips:

Add cayenne pepper if you want your shrimp spicier.

Nutritional Values (Per Serving)

Calories: 234

Fat: 45 g

Carbohydrates: 6 g

Protein: 23 g

Shrimp Boil

Preparation Time: 10 minutes

Cooking Time: 15 minutes

Servings: 6

INGREDIENTS:

12 oz. shrimp, peeled and deveined

14 oz. smoked sausage, sliced

4 corn on cobs, sliced into 4

3 cups potatoes, sliced in half and boiled

1/8 cup Old Bay seasoning

¼ cup white onion, diced

Cooking spray

DIRECTIONS:

Mix all the ingredients in the inner pot of the Ninja Foodi Grill.

Spray mixture with oil.

Set the unit to **Air Fry**.

Air fry at 390°F for 5-7 minutes.

Stir and cook for another 6 minutes.

Serving Suggestions:

Sprinkle with dried herbs before serving.

Preparation/Cooking Tips:

Check the dish halfway through cooking to see if it's cooking evenly.

Nutritional Values (Per Serving)

Calories: 267

Fat: 23 g

Carbohydrates: 10 g

Protein: 22 g

Salmon and Kale Meal

Preparation Time: 10 minutes

Cooking Time: 5 minutes

Servings: 4

INGREDIENTS:

1 lemon, juiced

2 salmon fillets

¼ cup extra virgin olive oil

1 teaspoon Dijon mustard

4 cups kale, thinly sliced, ribs removed

1 teaspoon salt

1 avocado, diced

1 cup pomegranate seeds

1 cup walnuts, toasted

1 cup goat parmesan cheese, shredded

DIRECTIONS:

Season salmon with salt and keep it on the side.

Place a trivet in your Ninja Foodi.

Place salmon over the trivet.

Lock the lid and cook on high pressure for 15 minutes.

Release pressure naturally over 10 minutes.

Transfer salmon to a serving platter.

Take a bowl and add kale, season with salt.

Take another bowl and make the dressing by adding lemon juice, Dijon mustard, olive oil, and red wine vinegar.

Season kale with dressing, and add diced avocado, pomegranate seeds, walnuts, and cheese.

Toss and serve with the fish.

Enjoy!

Nutritional Values (Per Serving)

Calories: 234

Fat: 14 g

Saturated Fat: 6 g

Carbohydrates: 12 g

Fiber: 2 g

Sodium: 118 mg

Protein: 16 g

Lemon and Garlic Flavored Prawn Dish

Preparation Time: 5 minutes

Cooking Time: 5 minutes

Servings: 4

INGREDIENTS:

1 pound prawns

2/3 cup fish stock

1 tablespoon butter

2 tablespoons olive oil

2 tablespoons garlic, minced

2 tablespoons lemon juice

1 tablespoon lemon zest

Salt and pepper to taste

DIRECTIONS:

Set your Ninja Foodi to Sauté mode.

Add oil and butter, let it heat up.

Stir in remaining ingredients.

Close the lid.

Cook for 5 minutes on Low.

Quick-release the pressure.

Serve and enjoy!

Nutritional Values (Per Serving)

Calories: 236 g

Fat: 12 g
Saturated Fat: 3 g
Carbohydrates: 2 g

Fiber: 1 g
Sodium: 964 mg
Protein: 27 g

Chapter 6: Pork and Other Red Meat Recipes

Korean Chili Pork

Preparation Time: 5-10 minutes

Cooking Time: 8 minutes

Servings: 4

INGREDIENTS:

2 pounds pork, cut into ⅛-inch slices

5 minced garlic cloves

3 tablespoons minced green onion

1 yellow onion, sliced

½ cup soy sauce

½ cup brown sugar

3 tablespoons Korean red chili paste or regular chili paste

2 tablespoons sesame seeds

3 teaspoons black pepper

Red pepper flakes to taste

DIRECTIONS:

Take a zip-lock bag, add all the ingredients. Shake well and refrigerate for 6-8 hours to marinate.

Take Ninja Foodi Grill, orchestrate it over your kitchen stage, and open the top.

Mastermind the barbecue mesh and close the top cover.

Click **Grill** and choose the **Med** grill function. flame broil work. Modify the clock to 8 minutes and press **Start/Stop.** Ninja Foodi will begin to warm up.

Ninja Foodi is preheated and prepared to cook when it begins to signal. After you hear a signal, open the top.

Fix finely sliced pork on the barbeque mesh.

Cover and cook for 4 minutes. Then open the cover, switch the side of the pork.

Cover it and cook for another 4 minutes.

Serve warm with chopped lettuce (optional).

NUTRITIONAL:

Calories: 621

Fat: 31 g

Saturated Fat: 12.5 g

Trans Fat: 0 g

Carbohydrates: 29 g

Fiber: 3 g

Sodium: 1428 mg

Protein: 53 g

Grilled Steak & Potatoes

Preparation Time: 20 minutes

Cooking Time: 50 minutes

Servings: 4

INGREDIENTS:

4 potatoes

3 sirloin steaks

¼ cup avocado oil

2 tablespoons steak seasoning

Salt to taste

DIRECTIONS:

Poke potatoes with a fork.

Coat potatoes with half of the avocado oil.

Season with salt.

Add to the air fryer basket.

Choose the air fry function in your Ninja Foodi Grill.

Seal the hood and cook at 400°F for 35 minutes.

Flip and cook for another 10 minutes.

Transfer to a plate.

Add the grill grate to the Ninja Foodi Grill.

Add steaks to the grill grate.

Set it to **High**.

Cook for 7 minutes per side.

Serve steaks with potatoes.

Serving Suggestions:

Serve with steak sauce and hot sauce.

Preparation/Cooking Tips:

Press steaks onto the grill to give it grill marks.

Nutritional Values (Per Serving)

Calories: 245

Fat: 26 g

Carbohydrates: 7 g

Protein: 19 g

Roast Beef with Garlic

Preparation Time: 15 minutes

Cooking Time: 1 hour and 20 minutes

Servings: 4

INGREDIENTS:

2 lb. beef roast, sliced

2 tablespoons vegetable oil

Salt and pepper to taste

6 cloves garlic

DIRECTIONS:

Coat beef roast with oil.

Season with salt and pepper.

Place them inside the Ninja Foodi Grill pot.

Sprinkle garlic on top.

Choose the **Bake** setting.

Set it to 400°F and cook for 30 minutes.

Reduce temperature to 375°F and cook for another 40 minutes.

Serving Suggestions:

Serve with mashed potato and gravy.

Preparation/Cooking Tips:

If refrigerated, let beef come to room temperature 2 hours before cooking.

Nutritional Values (Per Serving)

Calories: 390

Fat: 29 g

Carbohydrates: 5 g

Protein: 20 g

Generous Pesto Beef Meal

Preparation Time: 10 minutes

Cooking Time: 14 minutes

Servings: 4

INGREDIENTS:

½ teaspoon pepper

½ teaspoon salt

½ cup feta cheese, crumbled

2/3 cup pesto

½ cup walnuts, chopped

4 cups grape tomatoes, halved

4 cups penne pasta, uncooked

10 ounces baby spinach, chopped

4 beef (6 ounces each) tenderloin steaks

DIRECTIONS:

Cook the pasta according to the package instructions.

Drain the pasta and rinse it.

Keep the pasta on the side.

Season the tenderloin steaks with pepper and salt.

Preheat your Ninja Foodi Grill to **High,** and set the timer to 7 minutes.

You will hear a beep once the preheating sequence is complete.

Transfer steak to your grill and cook for 7 minutes, flip and cook for 7 minutes more.

Take a bowl and add pasta, walnuts, spinach, tomatoes, and pesto.

Mix well.

Garnish your steak with cheese and serve with the prepared sauce.

Enjoy!

Nutritional Values (Per Serving)

Calories: 361

Fat: 5 g

Saturated Fat: 1 g

Carbohydrates: 16 g

Fiber: 4 g

Sodium: 269 mg

Protein: 33 g

Authentic Korean Flank Steak

Preparation Time: 10 minutes

Cooking Time: 10minutes

Servings: 4

INGREDIENTS:

1 teaspoon red pepper flakes

½ cup and 1 tablespoon soy sauce

1½ pounds flank steak

¼ cup and 2 tablespoons vegetable oil

½ cup of rice wine vinegar

3 tablespoons sriracha

2 cucumbers, seeded and sliced

4 garlic cloves, minced

2 tablespoons ginger, minced

2 tablespoons honey

3 tablespoons sesame oil

1 teaspoon sugar

Salt to taste

DIRECTIONS:

Take a bowl and add ½ cup soy sauce, half of the rice wine, honey, ginger, garlic, 2 tablespoons sriracha, 2 tablespoons sesame oil, and vegetable oil.

Mix well, pour half of the mixture over steak and rub well.

Cover steak and let it sit for 10 minutes.

Prepare the salad mix by add remaining rice wine vinegar, sesame oil, sugar red pepper flakes, sriracha sauce, soy sauce, and salt in a salad bowl.

Preheat your Ninja Foodi Grill on High, with the timer set to 12 minutes.

Transfer steak to your Grill and cook for 6 minutes per side.

Slice and serve with the salad mix.

Enjoy!

Nutritional Values (Per Serving)

Calories: 327

Fat: 4 g

Saturated Fat: 0.5 g

Carbohydrates: 33 g

Fiber: 1 g

Sodium: 142 mg

Protein: 24 g

Garlic Butter Pork

Preparation Time: 10 minutes

Cooking Time: 20 minutes

Servings: 4

INGREDIENTS:

1 tablespoon coconut butter

1 tablespoon coconut oil

2 teaspoons cloves garlic, grated

2 teaspoons parsley

Salt and pepper to taste

4 pork chops, sliced into strips

DIRECTIONS:

Combine all the ingredients except the pork strips. Mix well.

Marinate the pork in the mixture for 1 hour. Put the pork on the Ninja Foodi basket.

Set it inside the pot. Seal with the crisping lid. Choose **Air Crisp**.

Cook at 400°F for 10 minutes.

Serving Suggestion:

Serve with a fresh garden salad.

Tips:

You can also use pork loin for this recipe.

Nutritional Information Per Serving:

Calories: 388

Total Fat: 23.3 g

Saturated Fat: 10.4 g

Cholesterol: 69 mg

Sodium: 57 mg

Total Carbohydrate: 0.5 g

Dietary Fiber: 0.1 g

Total Sugars: 0 g

Protein: 18.1 g

Potassium: 285 mg

Pork with Gravy

Preparation Time: 10 minutes

Cooking Time: 30minutes

Servings: 4

INGREDIENTS:

5 pork chops

1 tablespoon olive oil

1 teaspoon salt

½ teaspoon pepper

½ teaspoon garlic powder

2 cups beef broth

1 packet ranch dressing mix

10½ oz. cream of chicken soup

1 packet brown gravy mix

2 tablespoons corn starch dissolved in 2 tablespoons water

DIRECTIONS:

Season both sides of the pork chops with salt, pepper, and garlic powder.

Pour the olive oil into the Ninja Foodi. Set it to **Sauté**.

Brown the pork chops on both sides. Remove and set aside.

Pour the beef broth to deglaze the pot.

Add the rest of the ingredients except the corn starch. Seal the pot.

Set it to **Pressure**. Cook at high pressure for 8 minutes. Release the pressure naturally.

Remove the pork chops. Turn the pot to **Sauté**. Stir in the corn starch.

Simmer to thicken. Pour the gravy over the pork chops.

Serving Suggestion:

Serve with mashed potatoes.

Tips:

If cream of chicken is not available, you can also use cream of mushroom soup.

Nutritional Information Per Serving:

Calories: 357

Total Fat: 26.8 g

Saturated Fat: 9 g

Cholesterol: 74 mg

Sodium: 1308 mg

Total Carbohydrate: 6 g

Dietary Fiber: 0.1 g

Total Sugars: 0.8 g

Protein: 21.6 g

Potassium: 396 mg

Hawaiian Pork

Preparation Time: 10 minutes

Cooking Time: 20 minutes

Servings: 4

INGREDIENTS:

20 oz. pineapple chunks, undrained

2 tablespoons water

1 tablespoon corn starch

2 tablespoons soy sauce

3 tablespoons honey

1 tablespoon ginger, grated

2 tablespoons brown sugar

3 cloves garlic, minced

2 tablespoons olive oil, divided

1 onion, chopped

2 lb. pork stew meat

Salt and pepper to taste

1 teaspoon oregano

DIRECTIONS:

Mix the pineapple juice, soy sauce, honey, ginger, sugar, and garlic in a bowl. Set aside. Set the Ninja Foodi to **Sauté**. Add half of the oil. Cook the onion for 1 minute.

Add the remaining oil. Brown the pork on both sides.

Add the pineapple chunks, oregano, and pineapple juice mixture.

Cover the pot. Set it to **Pressure**. Cook on high pressure for 10 minutes.

Release the pressure naturally.

Serving Suggestion:

Garnish with chopped parsley.

Tips:

You can also add red pepper to this recipe.

Nutritional Information Per Serving:

Calories: 384

Total Fat: 27 g

Saturated Fat: 9 g

Cholesterol: 81 mg

Sodium: 317 mg

Total Carbohydrates: 13 g

Sugars: 10 g

Protein: 20 g

Potassium: 390 mg

Middle Eastern Lamb Stew

Preparation Time: 10 minutes

Cooking Time: 20 minutes

Servings: 4

INGREDIENTS:

2 tablespoons olive oil

1½ lb. lamb stew meat, sliced into cubes

1 onion, diced

6 garlic cloves, chopped

1 teaspoon cumin

1 teaspoon coriander

1 teaspoon turmeric

1 teaspoon cinnamon

Salt and pepper to taste

2 tablespoons tomato paste

¼ cup red wine vinegar

2 tablespoons honey

1¼ cups chicken broth

15 oz. chickpeas, rinsed and drained

¼ cup raisins

DIRECTIONS:

Choose **Sauté** on the Ninja Foodi. Add the oil. Cook the onion for 3 minutes.

Add the lamb and seasonings. Cook for 5 minutes, stirring frequently.

Stir in the rest of the ingredients. Cover the pot. Set it to **Pressure**.

Cook on high pressure for 50 minutes. Release the pressure naturally.

Serving Suggestion:

Serve with quinoa.

Tips:

Freeze and serve the next day for a more intense flavor.

Nutritional Information Per Serving:

Calories: 867

Total Fat: 26.6 g

Saturated Fat: 6.3 g

Cholesterol: 153 mg

Sodium: 406 mg

Total Carbohydrate: 87.4 g

Dietary Fiber: 20.4 g

Total Sugars: 27.9 g

Protein: 71.2 g

Potassium: 1815 mg

Lamb Curry

Preparation Time: 10 minutes

Cooking Time: 10minutes

Servings: 4

INGREDIENTS:

1½ lb. lamb stew meat, cubed

1 tablespoon lime juice

4 cloves garlic, minced

½ cup coconut milk

1-inch piece fresh ginger, grated

Salt and pepper to taste

1 tablespoon coconut oil

14 oz. diced tomatoes

¾ teaspoon turmeric

1 tablespoon curry powder

1 onion, diced

3 carrots, sliced

DIRECTIONS:

In a bowl, toss the lamb meat in lime juice, garlic, coconut milk, ginger, salt, and pepper. Marinate for 30 minutes.

Put the meat with its marinade and the rest of the ingredients into the Ninja Foodi.

Mix well. Seal the pot. Set it to **Pressure**. Cook at high pressure for 20 minutes.

Release the pressure naturally.

Serving Suggestion:

Garnish with chopped cilantro.

Tips:

Use freshly squeezed lime juice.

Nutritional Information Per Serving:

Calories: 631

Total Fat: 31.4 g

Saturated Fat: 18.4 g

Cholesterol: 204 mg

Sodium: 230 mg

Total Carbohydrate: 19.7 g

Dietary Fiber: 5.7 g

Total Sugars: 9.5 g

Protein: 67.2 g

Potassium: 1490 mg

Deliciously Smothered Pork Chops

Preparation Time: 10 minutes

Cooking Time: 28 minutes

Servings: 4

INGREDIENTS:

6 ounce of boneless pork loin chops

1 tablespoon of paprika

1 teaspoon of garlic powder

1 teaspoon of onion powder

1 teaspoon of black pepper

1 teaspoon of salt

¼ teaspoon of cayenne pepper

2 tablespoon of coconut oil

½ of a sliced medium onion

6-ounce baby Bella mushrooms, sliced

1 tablespoon of butter

½ a cup of whip cream

¼ teaspoon of xanthan gum

1 tablespoon parsley, chopped

DIRECTIONS:

Take a small bowl and add garlic powder, paprika, onion powder, black pepper, salt, and cayenne pepper.

Rinse the pork chops and pat them dry.

Sprinkle both sides with 1 teaspoon of the mixture, making sure to rub the seasoning all over the meat. Reserve the remaining spice.

Set your Ninja Foodi to **Sauté** and add coconut oil. Allow the oil to heat up.

Brown the chops, 3 minutes per side.

Remove and cancel the Sauté mode.

Add sliced onion to the base of your pot alongside mushrooms.

Top with the browned pork chops.

Lock the lid and cook on high pressure for 25 minutes.

Release the pressure naturally over 10 minutes. Remove the pork chops and keep them on a plate.

Set your pot to Sauté mode and whisk in remaining spices mix, heavy cream, and butter.

Sprinkle ¼ teaspoon of Xanthan gum and stir.

Simmer for 3-5 minutes and remove the heat.

Add a bit more Xanthan gum if you require a heavier gravy.

Top the pork chops with the gravy, and sprinkle parsley.

Serve!

Nutritional Values (Per Serving)

Calories: 481

Fat: 32g

Saturated Fat: 15 g

Carbohydrates: 6 g

Fiber: 2 g

Sodium: 210 mg

Protein: 39 g

Beef and Broccoli Meal

Preparation Time: 10 minutes

Cooking Time: 15 minutes

Servings: 4

INGREDIENTS:

1½ pounds beef round steak, cut into 2-inch by 1/8-inch strips

1 cup broccoli, diced

½ teaspoon red pepper flakes

2 teaspoon garlic, minced

2 teaspoons olive oil

2 tablespoons apple cider vinegar

2 tablespoons coconut aminos

2 tablespoons white wine vinegar

1 tablespoons arrowroot

¼ cup beef broth

DIRECTIONS:

Take a large-sized bowl and make the sauce by mixing in red pepper flakes, olive oil, coconut aminos, garlic, white wine vinegar, apple cider vinegar, broth, and arrowroot.

Mix well.

Add the mix to your Ninja Foodi.

Add beef and place a lid.

Cook on Slow Cook mode (low) for 6-8 hours.

Uncover just 30 minutes before end time and add broccoli, lock the lid again and let it finish.

Serve and enjoy!

Nutritional Values (Per Serving)

Calories: 208

Fat: 12 g

Saturated Fat: 14 g

Carbohydrates: 11 g

Fiber: 3 g

Sodium: 545 mg

Protein: 15 g

Hearty New York Strip

Preparation Time: 10 minutes

Cooking Time: 9 minutes

Servings: 4

INGREDIENTS:

24 ounces NY strip steak

½ teaspoon ground black pepper

1 teaspoon salt

DIRECTIONS:

Add steaks on a metal trivet, place it on your Ninja Foodi.

Season with salt and pepper.

Add 1 cup water to the pot.

Close the lid.

Cook for 1 minute on **High.**

Quick-release the pressure.

Place the air crisp lid on, and air crisp for 8 minutes for a medium-steak.

Serve and enjoy!

Nutritional Values (Per Serving)

Calories: 503

Fat: 46 g

Saturated Fat: 12 g

Carbohydrates: 1g

Fiber: 0 g

Sodium: 715 mg

Protein: 46 g

Mediterranean Lamb Roast

Preparation Time: 10 minutes

Cooking Time: 10minutes

Servings: 4

INGREDIENTS:

2 tablespoons olive oil

5 lb. leg of lamb

Salt and pepper to taste

1 teaspoon dried marjoram

3 cloves garlic, minced

1 teaspoon dried sage

1 teaspoon dried thyme

1 teaspoon ground ginger

1 bay leaf, crushed

2 cups broth

3 lb. potatoes, sliced into cubes

2 tablespoons arrowroot powder

1/3 cup water

DIRECTIONS:

Set the Ninja Foodi to **Sauté**. Pour in the olive oil. Add the lamb.

Coat with the oil. Season with the herbs and spices. Sear on both sides.

Pour in the broth. Add the potatoes. Close the pot. Set it to **Pressure**.

Cook at high pressure for 50 minutes. Release the pressure naturally.

Dissolve the arrowroot powder in water.

Stir in the diluted arrowroot powder into the cooking liquid.

Let sit for a few minutes before serving.

Serving Suggestion:

Serve with cauliflower rice.

Tips:

You can use flour or another thickener in place of the arrowroot powder.

Nutritional Information Per Serving:

Calories: 688

Total Fat: 24.8 g

Saturated Fat: 8.1 g

Cholesterol: 255 mg

Sodium: 417 mg

Total Carbohydrate: 27.7 g

Dietary Fiber: 4.2 g

Total Sugars: 2.2 g

Protein: 83.8 g

Potassium: 1705 mg

Braised Lamb Shanks

Preparation Time: 10 minutes

Cooking Time: 40 minutes

Servings: 4

INGREDIENTS:

2 tablespoons olive oil

4 lamb shanks

Salt and pepper to taste

4 cloves garlic, minced

¾ cup dry red wine

1 teaspoon dried basil

¾ teaspoon dried oregano

28 oz. crushed tomatoes

DIRECTIONS:

Turn the Ninja Foodi to **Sauté**. Add the oil. Season the lamb with salt and pepper.

Cook until brown. Remove and set aside. Add the garlic and cook for 15 seconds.

Pour in the wine. Simmer for 2 minutes. Stir in the basil, oregano, and tomatoes.

Put the lamb back in the pot. Seal the pot. Set it to **Pressure**.

Cook at high pressure for 45 minutes. Release the pressure naturally.

Serving Suggestion:

Serve over polenta.

Nutritional Information Per Serving:

Calories: 790

Total Fat: 31 g

Saturated Fat: 9.6 g

Cholesterol: 294 mg

Sodium: 632 mg

Total Carbohydrate: 18.3 g

Dietary Fiber 6.5 g

Total Sugars: 11.5 g

Protein: 96.8 g

Potassium: 1157 mg

Rosemary Lamb Chops

Preparation Time: 10 minutes

Cooking Time: 10 minutes

Servings: 4

INGREDIENTS:

3 lb. lamb chops

4 rosemary sprigs

Salt to taste

1 tablespoon olive oil

2 tablespoons butter

1 tablespoon tomato paste

1 cup beef stock

1 green onion, sliced

DIRECTIONS:

Season the lamb chops with rosemary, salt, and pepper.

Pour in the olive oil and add the butter to the Ninja Foodi. Set it to **Sauté**.

Add the lamb chops and cook for one minute per side. Add the rest of the ingredients.

Stir well. Cover the pot. Set it to **Pressure**. Cook at high pressure for 5 minutes.

Release the pressure naturally.

Serving Suggestion:

Serve with pickled onions.

Tips:

You can also use tomato sauce in place of tomato paste.

Nutritional Information Per Serving:

Calories: 484

Total Fat: 23 g

Saturated Fat: 8.8 g

Cholesterol: 214 mg

Sodium: 361 mg

Total Carbohydrate: 1.2 g

Dietary Fiber: 0.5 g

Total Sugars: 0.4 g

Protein: 64.4 g

Potassium: 824 mg

Tantalizing Beef Jerky

Preparation time: 10 minutes

Cooking time: 20 minutes

Servings: 8

INGREDIENTS:

½ pound beef, sliced into 1/8-inch-thick strips

½ cup of soy sauce

2 tablespoons Worcestershire sauce

2 teaspoons ground black pepper

1 teaspoon onion powder

½ teaspoon garlic powder

1 teaspoon salt

DIRECTIONS:

Add listed ingredient to a large-sized Ziploc bag. Seal it shut.

Shake well, leave it in the fridge overnight.

Lay strips on dehydrator trays, making sure not to overlap them.

Lock the air crisping lid and set the temperature to 135°F. Cook for 7 hours.

Store in an airtight container and enjoy!

Nutritional Values (Per Serving)

Calories: 62

Fat: 7 g

Carbohydrates: 2 g

Protein: 9 g

Beefed Up Spaghetti Squash

Preparation time: 5 minutes

Cooking time: 10-15 minutes

Servings: 8

INGREDIENTS:

2 pounds ground beef

1 medium spaghetti squash

32 ounces marinara sauce

3 tablespoons olive oil

DIRECTIONS:

Slice squash in half lengthwise and dispose of seeds.

Add trivet to your Ninja Foodi.

Add 1 cup water.

Arrange squash on the rack and lock the lid, cook on high pressure for 8 minutes.

Quick-release the pressure.

Remove from pot.

Clean the pot and set your Ninja Foodi to **Sauté**.

Add ground beef and add olive oil, and let it heat up.

Add ground beef and cook until slightly browned and cooked.

Separate strands from cooked squash and transfer to a bowl.

Add cooked beef, and mix with marinara sauce. Serve and enjoy!

Nutritional Values (Per Serving)

Calories: 174

Fat: 6 g

Carbohydrates: 5 g

Protein: 19 g

The Yogurt Lamb Skewers

Preparation Time: 10 minutes

Cooking Time: 16 minutes

Servings: 4

INGREDIENTS:

2 garlic cloves, minced

1 pack of 10 ounces couscous

1 tablespoon and 1 teaspoon cumin

2 lemons, juiced

1½ cup yogurt

Salt to taste

1½ pound lamb leg, boneless, cubed

Fresh ground black pepper

2 tomatoes, seeded and diced

½ small red onion, chopped

3 tablespoons olive oil

½ cucumber, seeded and diced

¼ cup finely chopped fresh parsley

¼ cup fresh mint, chopped

Lemon wedges to serve

DIRECTIONS:

Cook couscous following the package instructions, and fluff it up with a fork.

Whisk yogurt with garlic, cumin, lemon juice, salt, pepper in a large-sized bowl.

Add lamb, mix well to coat it.

Separate toss red onion, cucumber, tomatoes, parsley, mint, lemon juice, olive oil, salt, and couscous in a salad bowl.

Thread your seasoned lamb on 8 skewers and drizzle salt and pepper over them.

Preheat your Ninja Foodi Grill on **High**. Set the timer to 16 minutes.

Once you hear the beep, place 4 skewers on the grill.

Let it cook for 4 minutes per side.

Cook the remaining ones in a similar way.

Serve and enjoy!

Nutritional Values (Per Serving)

Calories: 417

Fat: 11 g

Saturated Fat: 5 g

Carbohydrates: 20 g

Fiber: 2 g

Sodium: 749 mg

Protein: 13 g

Grilled Pork Chops

Preparation Time: 10 minutes

Cooking Time: 15 minutes

Servings: 4

INGREDIENTS:

4 pork chops

Salt and pepper to taste

Barbecue sauce

DIRECTIONS:

Add the grill grate to your Ninja Foodi Grill.

Set it to **Grill**. Close the hood.

Preheat to **High** for 15 minutes.

Season pork chops with salt and pepper.

Add to the grill grates.

Grill for 8 minutes.

Flip and cook for another 7 minutes, brushing both sides with barbecue sauce.

Serving Suggestions: Let rest for 5 minutes before slicing and serving.

Preparation/Cooking Tips: You can also make your own barbecue sauce by mixing soy sauce, sugar or honey, lemon juice, and ketchup.

Nutritional Values (Per Serving)

Calories: 324

Fat: 30 g

Carbohydrates: 4 g

Protein: 23 g

Cuban Pork Chops

Preparation Time: 8 hours and 20 minutes

Cooking Time: 30 minutes

Servings: 4

INGREDIENTS:

4 pork chops

½ cup olive oil

8 cloves garlic, minced

1 cup orange juice

½ cup lime juice

1 teaspoon orange zest

1 teaspoon lime zest

¼ cup mint leaves, chopped

2 teaspoons dried oregano

2 teaspoons ground cumin

1 cup cilantro, chopped

DIRECTIONS:

Place pork chops in a shallow plate.

In another bowl, mix the remaining ingredients.

Take ¼ cup of the mixture and set aside.

Add the remaining mixture to the pork chops.

Cover and marinate in the refrigerator for 8 hours.

Add the grill grate to the Ninja Foodi Grill. Seal the hood.

Choose the **Grill** setting.

Set it to **High**. Set the time to 15 minutes.

Close the hood and cook for 15 minutes, flipping once.

Serving Suggestions: Let rest for 5 minutes before slicing and serving.

Preparation/Cooking Tips: You can also marinate only for 1 hour if you want a shorter preparation time.

Nutritional Values (Per Serving)

Calories: 236

Fat: 34 g

Carbohydrates: 7 g

Protein: 12 g

Lettuce Cheese Steak

Preparation Time: 5-10 minutes

Cooking Time: 16 minutes

Servings: 5-6

INGREDIENTS:

4 (8-ounce) skirt steaks

6 cups romaine lettuce, chopped

¾ cup cherry tomatoes halved

¼ cup blue cheese, crumbled

Ocean salt and ground black pepper

2 avocados, peeled and sliced

1 cup croutons

1 cup blue cheese dressing

DIRECTIONS:

Coat steaks with black pepper and salt.

Take Ninja Foodi Grill, mastermind it over your kitchen stage, and open the top. Organize the barbecue mesh and close the top.

Click **Grill** and the **High** functions. Change the clock to 8 minutes and press **Start/Stop**. Ninja Foodi will begin pre-warming.

Ninja Foodi is preheated and prepared to cook when it begins to blare. After you hear a blare, open the top cover.

Fix finely the 2 steaks on the barbeque mesh.

Close the top cover and cook for 4 minutes. Presently open the top cover, flip the steaks.

Close the top cover and cook for 4 additional minutes. Cook until the food thermometer comes to 165°F. Cook for 3-4 more minutes if needed. Grill the remaining steaks.

In a mixing bowl, add the lettuce, tomatoes, blue cheese, and croutons. Combine the ingredients to mix well with each other.

Serve the steaks warm with the salad mixture, blue cheese dressing, and avocado slices on top.

NUTRITIONAL:

Calories: 576

Fat: 21 g

Saturated Fat: 8.5 g

Trans Fat: 0 g

Carbohydrates: 23 g

Fiber: 6.5 g

Sodium: 957 mg

Protein: 53.5 g

Grilled Beef Burgers

Preparation Time: 5-10 minutes

Cooking Time: 10 minutes

Servings: 4

INGREDIENTS:

4 ounces cream cheese

4 slices bacon, cooked and crumbled

2 seeded jalapeño peppers, stemmed, and minced

½ cup shredded Cheddar cheese

½ teaspoon chili powder

¼ teaspoon paprika

¼ teaspoon ground black pepper

2 pounds ground beef

4 hamburger buns

4 slices pepper Jack cheese

Optional - Lettuce, sliced tomato, and sliced red onion

DIRECTIONS:

In a mixing bowl, combine the peppers, cheddar cheese, cream cheese, and bacon until well combined.

Prepare the ground beef into 8 patties. Add the cheese mixture onto four of the patties;

arrange a second patty on top of each to prepare four burgers. Press gently.

In another bowl, combine the chili powder, paprika, and pepper. Sprinkle the mixture onto the sides of the burgers.

Take Ninja Foodi Grill, organize it over your kitchen stage, and open the top cover.

Organize the flame broil mesh and close the top cover.

Press **Flame Broil** and select the **High** barbecue work. Change the clock to 4 minutes and afterward press **Start/Stop**. Ninja Foodi will begin pre-warming.

Ninja Foodi is preheated and prepared to cook when it begins to blare. After you hear a blare, open the top. Arrange the burgers over the grill grate.

Close the top lid, and allow it to cook until the timer reads zero. Cook for 3-4 more minutes, if needed.

Cook until the food thermometer reaches 145°F. Serve warm.

Serve warm with buns. Add your choice of toppings: pepper Jack cheese, lettuce, tomato, and red onion.

NUTRITIONAL:

Calories: 783

Fat: 38 g

Saturated Fat: 16 g

Trans Fat: 0 g

Carbohydrates: 25 g

Fiber: 3 g

Sodium: 1259 mg

Protein: 57.5 g

Chapter 7: Dessert

Chocolate Fudge

Preparation time: 15 minutes

Cooking time: 6 hours

Servings: 24

INGREDIENTS:

½ teaspoon organic vanilla extract

1 cup heavy whipping cream

2 ounces butter softened

2 ounces 70% dark chocolate, finely chopped

DIRECTIONS:

Select **Sauté** and **Md: Hi** on Ninja Foodi, and add vanilla and heavy cream. Sauté for 5 minutes at **Low**.

Sauté for 10 minutes, and add butter and chocolate.

Sauté for 2 minutes and pour this mixture into a serving dish.

Refrigerate it for some hours and serve.

NUTRITIONAL:

Calories: 292

Total Fat: 26.2 g

Saturated Fat: 16.3 g

Cholesterol: 100 mg

Sodium: 86 mg

Total Carbs: 8.2 g

Fiber: 0 g

Sugar: 6.6 g

Protein: 5.2 g

Lime Cheesecake

Preparation Time: 15 minutes

Cooking time: 30 minutes

Servings: 6

INGREDIENTS:

¼ cup plus 1 teaspoon Erythritol

8 ounces cream cheese, softened

1/3 cup Ricotta cheese

1 teaspoon fresh lime zest, grated

2 tablespoons fresh lime juice

½ teaspoon organic vanilla extract

2 organic eggs

2 tablespoons sour cream

DIRECTIONS:

In a bowl, add ¼ cup of Erythritol and remaining ingredients except for eggs and sour cream. With a hand mixer, beat on high speed until smooth.

Add the eggs and beat on low speed until well combined.

Transfer the mixture into a 6-inch greased springform pan evenly.

With a piece of foil, cover the pan.

In the pot of the Ninja Foodi, place 2 cups of water.

Arrange a reversible rack in the pot of Ninja Foodi.

Place the springform pan over the reversible rack.

Close the Ninja Foodi with the pressure lid and place the pressure valve to the **Seal** position.

Select **Pressure** and set it to **High** for 30 minutes.

Press **Start/Stop** to begin cooking.

Switch the valve to Vent and do a Natural release.

Place the pan onto a wire rack to cool slightly.

Meanwhile, in a small bowl, add the sour cream and remaining Truvia and beat until well combined.

Spread the cream mixture on the warm cake evenly.

Refrigerate for about 6-8 hours before serving.

NUTRITIONAL:

Calories: 182

Fats: 16.6 g

Net Carbs: 2.1 g

Carbs: 2.1 g

Fiber: 0 g

Sugar: 0.3 g

Proteins: 6.4 g

Sodium: 152 mg

Baked Apples

Preparation Time: 15 minutes

Cooking Time: 45 minutes

Servings: 4

INGREDIENTS:

2 apples, sliced in half

1 tablespoon lemon juice

4 teaspoons brown sugar

¼ cup butter, sliced into small cubes

DIRECTIONS:

Add the crisper plate to the air fryer basket inside the Ninja Foodi Grill.

Choose the Air Fry function.

Preheat it to 325°F for 3 minutes.

Add apples to the crisper plate.

Drizzle with lemon juice and sprinkle with brown sugar.

Place butter cubes on top.

Air fry for 45 minutes.

Serving Suggestions: Top with caramel syrup or crushed graham crackers.

Preparation/Cooking Tips: Poke apples with a fork before cooking.

Nutritional Values (Per Serving)

Calories: 234

Fat: 17 g

Carbohydrates: 4 g

Protein: 21 g

Strawberry & Cake Kebabs

Preparation Time: 15 minutes

Cooking Time: 6 minutes

Servings: 5

INGREDIENTS:

1 pack white cake mix

2 cups strawberries, sliced in half

2 tablespoons honey

¼ cup sugar

Cooking spray

DIRECTIONS:

Cook cake mix according to the directions in the box.

Insert the grill grate in the Ninja Foodi Grill.

Choose the **Grill** setting.

Preheat at 325°F for 15 minutes.

While waiting, slice the cake into cubes.

Toss strawberries in honey and sugar.

Thread cake cubes and strawberries alternately onto skewers.

Grill for 3 minutes per side.

Serving Suggestions: Serve with vanilla ice cream.

Preparation/Cooking Tips: When preparing the cake mix, you can replace water with pudding to make the cake thicker.

Nutritional Values (Per Serving)

Calories: 234

Fat: 17 g

Carbohydrates: 5 g

Protein: 28 g

Mozzarella Sticks and Grilled Eggplant

Preparation Time: 10 minutes

Cooking Time: 14 minutes

Servings: 4

INGREDIENTS:

Salt as needed

½ pound buffalo mozzarella, sliced into ¼-inch thick

12 large basil leaves

2 heirloom tomatoes, sliced into ¼ inch thickness

2 tablespoon canola oil

1 eggplant, ¼-inch thick

DIRECTIONS:

Take a large bowl and add the eggplant, add oil and toss well until coated well.

Preheat your Ninja Foodi to MAX and set the timer to 15 minutes.

Once you hear the beeping sound, transfer the prepared eggplants to your Grill and cook for 8-12 minutes until the surface is charred.

Top with cheese slice, tomato, and mozzarella.

Cook for 2 minutes, letting the cheese melt.

Remove from grill and place 2-3 basil leaves on top of half stack.

Place remaining eggplant stack on top alongside basil.

Season well with salt and the rest of the basil.

Enjoy!

Nutritional Values (Per Serving)

Calories:

Fat: 19 g

Saturated Fat: 19 g

Carbohydrates: 11 g

Fiber: 4 g

Sodium: 1555 mg

Protein: 32 g

Almond Cherry Bars

Preparation time: 5 minutes

Cooking time: 35 minutes

Servings: 12

INGREDIENTS:

Xanthan gum, 1 tbsp.

Almond flour, 1 ½ cup

Salt, ½ tsp

Pitted fresh cherries, 1 cup

Softened butter, ½ cup

Eggs, 2

Water, ¼ cup

Vanilla, ½ tsp

Erythritol, 1 cup

DIRECTIONS:

Combine almond flour, softened butter, salt, vanilla, eggs, and erythritol in a large bowl until you form a dough.

Press the dough in a baking dish that will fit in the air fryer.

Set in the air fryer and bake for 10 minutes at 375°F.

Meanwhile, mix the cherries, water, and xanthan gum in a bowl.

Take the dough out and pour over the cherry mixture.

Cook again for 25 minutes more at 375°F in the air fryer.

NUTRITIONAL: Calories: 99; Carbs: 2.1 g; Fat: 9.3 g; Protein: 1.8 g

Coffee Flavored Doughnuts

Preparation time: 5 minutes

Cooking time: 6 minutes

Servings: 6

INGREDIENTS:

Baking powder 1 tsp.

Salt ½ tsp.

Sunflower oil 1 tbsp.

Coffee ¼ cup

Coconut sugar ¼ cup

White all-purpose flour 1 cup

Aquafaba 2 tbsp

DIRECTIONS:

Combine sugar, flour, baking powder, salt in a mixing bowl.

In another bowl, combine the aquafaba, sunflower oil, and coffee.

Mix to form a dough.

Let the dough rest inside the fridge.

Preheat the air fryer to 400°F.

Knead the dough and create doughnuts.

Arrange inside the air fryer in a single layer and cook for 6 minutes.

Do not shake so that the donut maintains its shape.

NUTRITIONAL: Calories: 113; Protein: 2.16 g; Fat: 2.54 g; Carbs: 20.45 g

Ginger Cheesecake

Preparation time: 2 hours and 10 minutes

Cooking time: 20 minutes

Servings: 6

INGREDIENTS:

Ground nutmeg ½ tsp.

Soft cream cheese 16 oz.

Rum 1 tsp.

Crumbled ginger cookies ½ cup

Vanilla extract ½ tsp.

Melted butter 2 tsp.

Eggs 2.

Sugar ½ cup

DIRECTIONS:

Grease a pan with butter and spread cookie crumbs on the bottom.

In a bowl, beat cream cheese, eggs, rum, vanilla, and nutmeg. Whisk well and spread over the cookie crumbs.

Place in the air fryer and cook at 340°F for 20 minutes.

Cool and keep in the refrigerator.

Slice and serve.

NUTRITIONAL: Calories: 412; Fat: 12 g; Protein: 6 g; Carbs: 20 g

Pork Taquitos

Preparation time: 10 minutes

Cooking time: 10 minutes

Servings: 4

INGREDIENTS:

Small whole-wheat tortillas 10.

Shredded mozzarella cheese 2 ½ cup

Cooked and shredded pork tenderloin 30 oz.

Lime juice 1 lime

DIRECTIONS:

Preheat your air fryer to 380°F.

Stir the lime juice over the shredded pork tenderloins.

Soften the tortillas in your air fryer by microwaving it for 10 seconds.

For each tortilla, add 3-ounces of the shredded pork and ¼ cup of the mozzarella cheese.

Lightly roll up the tortillas.

Then spray a nonstick cooking spray over the tortillas and place it inside your air fryer.

Cook it for 10 minutes or until it gets a golden-brown color, as you flip after 5 minutes, then serve and enjoy.

NUTRITIONAL: Calories: 210; Fat: 29 g; Protein: 7 g; Carbs: 15 g

Crusted Mozzarella Sticks

Preparation time: 15 minutes

Cooking time: 5 minutes

Servings: 12

INGREDIENTS:

Italian seasoning, 1 tsp.

Beaten large eggs, 2.

Garlic salt, ½ tsp.

Halved mozzarella sticks string cheese, 12.

Parmesan cheese, ½ cup

Almond flour, ½ cup

DIRECTIONS:

Mix almond flour with Italian seasoning, garlic salt, and parmesan cheese.

Whisk eggs in a separate bowl and keep them aside.

Dip the mozzarella sticks in eggs then coat with cheese mixture.

Arrange them on a well-lined baking tray with wax paper.

Freeze the sticks for 30 minutes, then place them in the air fryer basket.

Ground ginger, ½ tsp.

Egg whites, 4.

DIRECTIONS:

Let your air fryer preheat to 400°F.

Meanwhile, toss the chicken cubes with sesame oil and salt.

Mix coconut flour with ground ginger in a Ziploc bag then place the chicken in it.

Zip the bag and shake well to coat the chicken well.

Whisk egg whites in a bowl, then dip the coated chicken in egg whites.

Coat them with sesame seeds and shake off the excess.

Place the nuggets in the air fryer basket and return the basket to the fryer.

Air fry the nuggets for 6 minutes, then flip them.

Spray the nuggets with cooking oil and cook for another 6 minutes.

Serve fresh.

NUTRITIONAL:

Calories: 130; Fat: 10.3 g; Carbs: 9 g; Protein: 74.7 g

Simple Strawberry Cobbler

Preparation time: 10 minutes

Cooking time: 25 minutes

Servings: 4

INGREDIENTS:

Heavy whipping cream, ¼ cup

Cornstarch, 1 ½ tsp.

White sugar, ¼ cup

Water, ½ cup

Salt, ¼ tsp.

Butter, 2 tsp.

Hulled strawberries, 1 ½ cup

White sugar, 1 ½ tsp.

Diced butter, 1 tbsp.

Butter, 1 tbsp.

All-purpose flour, ½ cup

Baking powder, ¾ tsp.

DIRECTIONS:

Lightly grease the baking pan of the air fryer with cooking spray. Add water, cornstarch, and sugar. Cook for 10 minutes 3900F or until hot and thick. Add strawberries and mix well. Dot the top with 1 tablespoon butter.

In a bowl, mix well salt, baking powder, sugar, and flour. Cut in 1 tablespoon and 2 teaspoons butter. Mix in cream. Spoon on top of berries.

Cook for 15 minutes at 390°F, until the top is lightly browned.

Serve and enjoy.

NUTRITIONAL:

Calories: 255; Protein: 2.4 g; Fat: 13.0 g; Carbs: 32.0 g

Cheesy Cauliflower Steak

Preparation Time: 10 minutes

Cooking Time: 30 minutes

Servings: 4

INGREDIENTS:

1 tablespoon mustard

1 head cauliflower

1 teaspoon avocado mayonnaise

½ cup parmesan cheese, grated

¼ cup butter, cut into small pieces

DIRECTIONS:

Set your Ninja Foodi to **Sauté** mode, and add butter and cauliflower.

Sauté for 3 minutes.

Add remaining ingredients and stir.

Lock the lid and cook on High pressure for 30 minutes.

Release pressure naturally over 10 minutes.

Serve and enjoy!

Nutritional Values (Per Serving)

Calories: 155

Fat: 13g

Saturated Fat: 2 g

Carbohydrates: 4 g

Fiber: 2 g

Sodium: 162 mg

Protein: 6 g

Garlic and Mushroom Munchies

Preparation Time: 10 minutes

Cooking Time: 8 hours

Servings: 4

INGREDIENTS:

¼ cup vegetable stock

2 tablespoons extra virgin olive oil

1 tablespoon Dijon mustard

1 teaspoon dried thyme

1 teaspoon of sea salt

½ teaspoon dried rosemary

¼ teaspoon fresh ground black pepper

2 pounds cremini mushrooms, cleaned

6 garlic cloves, minced

¼ cup fresh parsley, chopped

DIRECTIONS:

Take a small bowl and whisk in vegetable stock, mustard, olive oil, salt, thyme, pepper, and rosemary.

Add mushrooms, garlic, and stock mix to your Ninja Foodi.

Close lid and cook on Slow Cook mode (low) for 8 hours.

Open the lid and stir in parsley.

Serve and enjoy!

Nutritional Values (Per Serving)

Calories: 92

Fat: 5 g

Saturated Fat: 2 g

Carbohydrates: 8 g

Fiber: 2 g

Sodium: 550 mg

Protein: 4 g

Warm Glazed Up Carrots

Preparation Time: 5 minutes

Cooking Time: 5 minutes

Servings: 4

INGREDIENTS:

2 pounds carrots

Pepper as needed

1 cup of water

1 tablespoon coconut butter

DIRECTIONS:

Wash carrots thoroughly and peel then, slice the carrots.

Add carrots, water to the Ninja Foodi.

Lock pressure lid and cook for 4 minutes on High pressure.

Release pressure naturally.

Strain carrots and strain carrots.

Mix with coconut butter, enjoy with a bit of pepper.

Nutritional Values (Per Serving)

Calories: 228

Fat: 8 g

Saturated Fat: 2 g

Carbohydrates: 36 g

Fiber: 2 g

Sodium: 123 mg

Protein: 4 g

Great Mac and Cheese Bowl

Preparation Time: 10 minutes

Cooking Time: 10 minutes

Servings: 4

INGREDIENTS:

1 tablespoon parmesan cheese, grated

Salt and pepper to taste

1½ cup cheddar cheese, grated

½ cup warm milk

½ cup broccoli

1 cup elbow macaroni

DIRECTIONS:

Preheat your Ninja Foodi to 400°F in Air Crisp mode, set a timer to 10 minutes.

Once you hear the beep, it is preheated.

Take a pot and add water, bring the water to a boil.

Add macaroni and veggies, boil for 10 minutes until cooked.

Drain pasta and veggies, toss pasta and veggies with cheese and sauce.

Season well with salt and pepper and transfer to Ninja Foodi.

Sprinkle more cheese on top and cook for 15 minutes.

Take it out and let it cool for 10 minutes.

Serve and enjoy!

Nutritional Values (Per Serving)

Calories: 180

Fat: 11 g

Saturated Fat: 3 g

Carbohydrates: 14 g

Fiber: 3 g

Sodium: 287 mg

Protein: 6 g

The Healthy Granola Bites

Preparation Time: 10 minutes

Cooking Time: 15-20 minutes

Servings: 4

INGREDIENTS:

Salt and pepper to taste

1 tablespoon coriander

A handful of thyme, diced

¼ cup of coconut milk

3 handful of cooked vegetables, your choice

3-ounce plain granola

DIRECTIONS:

Preheat your Ninja Foodi to 352°F in Air Crisp mode, set a timer to 20 minutes.

Take a bowl and add your cooked vegetables, granola.

Use an immersion blender to blitz your granola until you have a nice breadcrumb-like consistency.

Add coconut milk to the mix and mix until you have a nice firm texture.

Use the mixture to make granola balls and transfer them to your Grill.

Cook for 20 minutes.

Serve and enjoy!

Nutritional Values (Per Serving)

Calories: 140

Fat: 10 g

Saturated Fat: 3 g

Carbohydrates: 14 g

Fiber: 4 g

Sodium: 215 mg

Protein: 2 g

Grilled Donuts

Preparation Time: 15 minutes

Cooking Time: 10 minutes

Servings: 8

INGREDIENTS:

¼ cup milk

1 teaspoon vanilla extract

2 cups powdered sugar

16 oz. prepared biscuit dough

Cooking spray

DIRECTIONS:

In a bowl, mix milk, vanilla, and sugar.

Cut rings from the prepared dough.

Refrigerate for 5 minutes.

Add the grill grate to the Ninja Foodi Grill.

Choose the **Grill** setting.

Set it to **Medium**.

Preheat for 6 minutes.

Spray round dough with oil.

Add to the grill and cook for 4 minutes.

Dip in the milk mixture and grill for another 4 minutes.

Serving Suggestions: Sprinkle with cinnamon sugar or chocolate sprinkles before serving.

Nutritional Values (Per Serving)

Calories: 128

Fat: 18 g

Carbohydrates: 5 g

Protein: 24 g

Lemon Cheesecake

Preparation Time: 15 minutes

Cooking time: 4 hours

Servings: 12

INGREDIENTS:

For the Crust:

1½ cups almond flour

4 tablespoons butter, melted

3 tablespoons sugar-free peanut butter

3 tablespoons Erythritol

1 large organic egg, beaten

For Filling:

1 cup ricotta cheese

24 ounces cream cheese, softened

1½ cups Erythritol

2 teaspoons liquid Stevia

1/3 cup heavy cream

2 large organic eggs

3 large organic egg yolks

1 tablespoon fresh lemon juice

1 tablespoon organic vanilla extract

DIRECTIONS:

Grease the pot of Ninja Foodi.

For the crust: in a bowl, add all the ingredients and mix until well combined.

In the pot of prepared of Ninja Foodi, place the crust mixture and press to smooth the top surface.

With a fork, prick the crust at many places.

For the filling: in a food processor, add the ricotta cheese and pulse until smooth.

In a large bowl, add the ricotta, cream cheese, Erythritol, and Stevia, and with an electric mixer, beat over medium speed until smooth.

In another bowl, add the heavy cream, eggs, egg yolks, lemon juice, and vanilla extract and beat until well combined.

Add the egg mixture into cream cheese mixture and beat over medium speed until just combined.

Place the filling mixture over the crust evenly.

Close the Ninja Foodi with the crisping lid and select **Slow Cooker**.

Set on **Low** for 3-4 hours.

Press **Start/Stop** to begin cooking.

Place the pan onto a wire rack to cool.

Refrigerate to chill for at least 6-8 hours before serving.

NUTRITIONAL:

Calories: 410

Fats: 37.9 g

Net Carbs: 5.1 g

Carbs: 6.9 g

Fiber: 1.8 g

Sugar: 1.3 g

Proteins: 13 g

Sodium: 260 mg

Strawberry Crumble

Preparation Time: 15 minutes

Cooking time: 2 hours

Servings: 5

INGREDIENTS:

1 cup almond flour

2 tablespoons butter, melted

8-10 drops liquid Stevia

3-4 cups fresh strawberries, hulled and sliced

1 tablespoon butter, chopped

DIRECTIONS:

Lightly, grease the pot of Ninja Foodi.

In a bowl, add the flour, melted butter, and Stevia and mix until a crumbly mixture form.

In the pot of the prepared Ninja Foodi, place the strawberry slices and dot with chopped butter.

Spread the flour mixture on top evenly.

Close the Ninja Foodi with the crisping lid and select **Slow Cooker**.

Set on **Low** for 2 hours.

Press **Start/Stop** to begin cooking.

Place the pan onto a wire rack to cool slightly.

NUTRITIONAL:

Calories: 233 g

Fats: 19.2 g

Net Carbs: 6.6 g

Carbs: 10.7 g

Fiber: 4.1 g

Sugar: 5 g

Proteins: 0.7 g

Sodium: 50 mg

Cashew Cream

Preparation time: 18 minutes

Cooking Time: 10 minutes

Servings: 10

INGREDIENTS:

3 cups cashews

2 cups chicken stock

1 teaspoon salt

1 tablespoon butter

2 tablespoons ricotta cheese

DIRECTIONS:

Combine the cashews with the chicken stock in the Multicooker.

Add salt and close the multicooker lid. Cook the dish on **Pressure** mode for 10 minutes.

Remove the cashews from the multicooker and drain the nuts from the water. Transfer the cashews to a blender and add the ricotta cheese and butter.

Blend the mixture until it is smooth. When you get the texture you want, remove it from a blender. Serve it immediately or keep the cashew butter in the refrigerator.

NUTRITIONAL:

Calories: 252

Fat: 20.6 g

Carbs: 13.8 g

Protein: 6.8 g

CONCLUSION

This cookbook tried to offer you a large array of recipes using a new cooking appliance; the revolutionary Ninja Foodi, which combines pressure cookers, air fryers, ovens, and dehydrator at the same time. If you haven't heard about the Ninja Foodi, you should read this book, because not only will it offer some of the most sumptuous recipes that you can ever stumble into, but it will also offer you useful information that will help you understand the function of this new cooking appliance. So, if you are a newbie in using Ninja Foodi, don't get frustrated, because you will just find everything you need and enough information that will help you understand this cooking appliance better in this book.

If you have made a purchase of Ninja Foodi lately, you shouldn't be afraid because with the help of this book; you will be able to master the use of this revolutionary cooking appliance. Besides this book will offer you some of the most important tips that may help you using Ninja Foodi perfectly from the first use.

If you have any doubts about this cooking appliance because it is new, and you don't have so much information about it. All you have to do is to download your copy of this book right away because it will clear out any types of ambiguity you have. Get ready to read this book because it will offer you a mixture of everything you need to learn about Ninja Foodi, its benefits, use, and more.

So, if you have made your purchase of Ninja Foodi lately, you shouldn't be afraid. With the help of this book you will be able to master the use of this revolutionary cooking appliance. Besides this book will offer you some of the most important tips that may help you use Ninja Foodi perfectly from the first use.

Thereby, with the introduction of the Ninja Pressure cookers to your kitchen and the world; you can discover for yourself a culinary revolution that has affected the kitchen. Ninja Foodi has, indeed, been considered as a more impressive kitchen appliance that many conventional cooking gadgets and appliances. All the people who have tried using Ninja Foodi find it more impressive and very easy to use. What most people like about the Ninja Foodi is that it can act as an air fryer, a pressure cooker, a roaster, a slow cooker, a steamer, a dehydrator, and more.

CPSIA information can be obtained
at www.ICGtesting.com
Printed in the USA
LVHW060141200321
681921LV00006BA/208